Carlisle (Citadel) Railway Scene

1   The main departure platforms at Citadel Station looking north.

CARLISLE (CITADEL) RAILWAY SCENE

C. C. Dorman

London
GEORGE ALLEN & UNWIN LTD
Ruskin House   Museum Street

Printed in Great Britain
in 11 point Plantin type
Cox and Wyman Ltd
London, Fakenham and Reading

Acknowledgements

The author and publishers wish to thank the following for permission to reproduce their photographs.

P. M. Alexander for plates 33, 43 and 93; British Railways for plates 5, 7, 26, 30, 54, 55, 56, 57, 60, 61, 63, 65, 97, 112, 113 and 114; Carlisle Public Library for plates 2, 3, 4, 15, 18 and 52; Carr and Co. for plates 40, 41 and 51; H. C. Casserley for plates 24, 31, 37, 38, 44, 55, 70, 74, 77, 78, 79, 92, 107 and 117; W. A. Corkhill for plate 94; M. W. Earley for plate 12; Locomotive and General Railway Photographs for plates 6, 14, 20 and 58; Locomotive Publishing Company for plate 72; C. A. J. Nevett for plates 73 and 90; Real Photographs Company for plates 6, 19, 25, 66, 71, 75, 80, 81, 82, 83, 84, 85, 86, 88, 89, 91, 95, 96, 98, 99, 100, 101, 102, 103, 104, 105, 106, 108, 109, 110, 111, 115 and 116; H. G. Tidey for plates 10, 11, 16, 17, 21, 23, 27, 28, 32, 34, 35, 36, 39, 45, 47, 48, 50, 64, 67, 68 and 76; J. L. Weston Collection for plates 1, 22, 29, 43, 44, 46, 49 and 54.

The author is also particularly grateful to Mr Derek Cross, who is well known for his excellent photographs of the area, for his help and guidance in the preparation of this book.

Contents

Illustrations

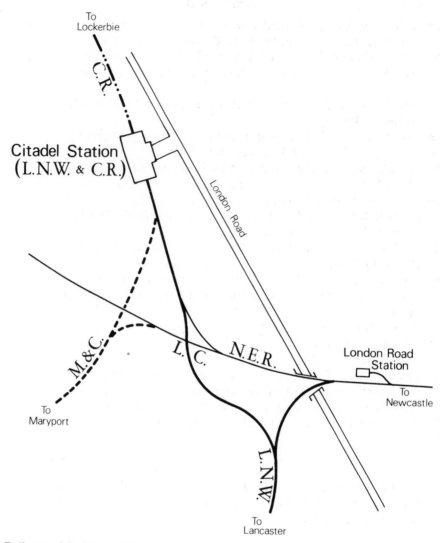

To
Lockerbie

C.R.

Citadel Station
(L.N.W. & C.R.)

London Road

London Road
Station

M&C.

L.C.   N.E.R.

To
Newcastle

To
Maryport

L.N.W.

To
Lancaster

I The Railways of Carlisle in 1854

Carlisle (Citadel) Railway Station

This brief pictorial history of Citadel Station may be enhanced by an even briefer glimpse of the history of the city itself. Carlisle dominates the North West of England just as its castle once dominated the route to Scotland. A Celtic settlement existed there for many years but virtually nothing is known of this period and the recorded history begins with the arrival of Agricola in AD 78. Since that time, Carlisle has been the scene of battles and border raids, and warfare was carried on longer in that region than anywhere else in England. In fact it only became an English city in 1092, having been previously granted to Malcolm, King of the Scots, in 945. Since that date, it has been temporarily recaptured by the Scots three times, the last occasion being, of course, the incursion of Bonnie Prince Charlie in 1745.

On leaving the Station on foot, the Citadel is immediately and magnificently visible to one's left, at the head of Botchergate. The building of the Castle (and the city walls) began in 1092 during the reign of William Rufus. At that time it was almost certainly a palisaded wooden structure; in its present form it dates from the early part of the fifteenth century. The Border Regiment (remember No. 6136, the Royal Scot class locomotive of this name) has always regarded Carlisle Castle as its 'home' and this was confirmed when the Regiment was granted the freedom of the City in 1960. Since the population of Carlisle is approximately 70,000 today, the city has some claim to railway economic interest apart from its great importance as a junction. However, it is fundamentally from the latter view that it used to be of such absorbing interest to the railway enthusiast. The surrounding countryside, with

2   Front elevation of the General Station, Court-Square, Carlisle (Mr Tite, architect).

3   An early photograph of the Court Houses at Carlisle.

the fells of the Northern Pennines nearby, with Keswick but an hour away to the south, the beautiful Solway Firth, and the glorious hills and moors of the Cheviots to the north and east, is a superb blend of Scottish and English scenery. Every train entering the city – from whichever direction – passes through fascinating scenery and it would be churlish to stress one line rather than any other. However, bearing this in mind, perhaps the Midland and North British lines of approach may be singled out as quite exceptionally beautiful. The British countryside has always seemed to take the railway to its heart. Embankments and cuttings alike are soon covered with grass and wild flowers, and lichen covers the rocky outcrops. The trains themselves seem at home in their surroundings – whether it be a Jubilee in the magnificent setting of Shap, or the seemingly weary Cauliflower panting up the hill to Troutbeck!

Stations in the area are generally modest buildings of local stone, i.e. slate in the fells, limestone or sandstone in the river valleys, and some Eskdale granite along the coast. But be that as it may; this book is concerned only with the railways of Carlisle.

A brief description of the colours discernible within the Station, when I first saw it in 1921, may give some impression of a scene so soon to pass into history. It was surely the grandest railway show on earth! Firstly, of course, the Premier Line: its locomotives in those days were invariably of sparkling blackberry black, lined with red and lunar white, with polished brass nameplates; the North Western carriages were of a rich chocolate with spilt milk upper panels. Their Scottish partners, the

4   The interior of Citadel Station in late Victorian times.

Caledonian, provided those magnificent blue engines whilst their passenger coaches were similar to the London and North Western except that the 'chocolate' had a vague auburn tinge. The Midland provided the beautiful crimson lake locomotives, with their superb carriages in similar colour, with clerestory roofs in leaden grey and crimson side decks. The N.B.R. locomotives were a very dark yellow and their carriages were purple-red, whilst their G.S.W.R. rivals from St Enoch were a middle green, with carriages very like their Midland partners. The North Eastern passenger engines were a bright sparkling green, with black under-frames, their coaches a rich plum red with brown roofs. Lastly, in their bay, was the Maryport and Carlisle contribution to the colourful scene, green engines and green and cream coaches.

All this began to change in 1923 when Carlisle became a two-company station, i.e. L.M.S.R. and L.N.E.R.; and subsequent visits were never quite so interesting, in spite of the advent of the Scots and the Princesses and Duchesses and the North Eastern Pacifics. However, there were still some sights which gladdened the heart of the enthusiast; for instance I remember seeing the departure of the 12.15 p.m. for Birmingham due into Crewe (first stop) at 3.36 p.m. with George V class 4-4-0 No. 789 *Windermere* piloting Claughton No. 30 *Thalaba* at the head of a sixteen-coach train, which included two dining cars; I'm sure *Windermere* could

5   A view of the forecourt at Citadel Station in the early 1920s.

have been heard on the lake she was named after! This, of course, was just after the introduction of the Royal Scots, when piloting on this section was gradually being dispensed with; but I have experienced instances of Jubilees and their like being piloted by the L.M.S.R.-built class 2 4–4–0s where the pilot engine was obviously working flat-out throughout the journey. Carlisle firemen were a notably hardy breed of men! However, enough of engines and enginemen for the moment. We are considering the Citadel and mention must be made of the excellent refreshment rooms within the Station, and the hotel just outside called the 'County', which was completed in 1853 and still flourishes.

Since 1877 Citadel Station has been free of goods traffic. In that year the avoiding lines were built which bypass Citadel to the west. These were operated jointly by all the major companies involved at Carlisle. The Station itself was completely rebuilt in 1880 at a cost of almost £500,000, and since that time very few fundamental alterations have been made. In 1899 electric lighting replaced the gas lamps, so prominent in old photographs of the station. It must surely have been one of the most fascinating stations in Britain and even today must be of great interest to the modern sophisticated railway enthusiast.

To sum up this brief description of the city and its station, it is notable that Carlisle, whilst it has every qualification to do so, has never degenerated into a 'museum' city. It remains as it has been for a thousand years – a very much alive, thrusting and exciting place, whilst continuing to be an important Border town of much interest to its many visitors. There is no doubt that the railways have been a prominent factor in the growth of the city.

6 L.N.W.R. No. 20, name engine of the 'John Hick' class, stands on the centre line at Citadel in 1894. Alongside is C.R. No. 71.

7   All that now remains of the original Station – the west side retaining wall for the overall roof.

Part One

CARLISLE BEFORE NATIONALISATION

Chapter 1

The London and North Western Railway

The first suggestions for a railway to Carlisle came from a mixed group of far-sighted men, engineers and aristocrats, in 1835, when there were no lines in operation north of Wigan. They envisaged a great trunk route from Lancaster to Glasgow and Edinburgh.

In 1846, after many vicissitudes, the Lancaster to Carlisle section of their dream came into being, and on 17 December of that year the public service began with two up and two down trains daily. The following year the first night mail train commenced. The locomotives used were 2-2-2s and 2-4-0s of the Trevithic-Allan standard Crewe types and the names of the first twelve were *Lonsdale, Belted Will, Dalemain, Greystoke, Wordsworth, Windermere, Saddleback, Eden, Lune, Bela, Lowther* and *Helvellyn*. To anyone who has made the journey over Shap hauled by a relatively modern steam engine, the thought of these tiny locomotives battling over

8   L.N.W.R. signals affixed to the north end of the station buildings on Platform 1.

the fells must surely be incredible. In the first year of operation, the Lancaster and Carlisle were allowed to use the Newcastle and Carlisle station at London Road since the joint Citadel Station did not open until September 1847. The following year the West Coast joint line from Euston to Glasgow Central may be said to have been established with the arrival of through-Caledonian trains. Prior to this, the Euston traveller to Scotland had to journey by train to Fleetwood, thence by ship to Ardrossan (on the Clyde coast) and finally by Caledonian train to Glasgow.

In 1859 the L.N.W.R. finally absorbed the Lancaster and Carlisle, and thereby re-absorbed the locomotives they had initially supplied the company from Crewe. These included named engines with local connections, such as *Luck of Edenhall, Skiddaw, Shap* and *Merrie Carlisle*, and the names were later perpetuated, as was the practice of the North Western throughout its existence. In 1875 the L.N.W.R., anticipating a massive growth in traffic from the south, abolished the old level-crossing with the North Eastern, just before the Crown Street bridge, with its superbly designed flying junctions. This crossing had been the scene of an accident in 1870 which cost six lives: a North Eastern goods train cut across and into a Scotch Express, due to the complete disregard of the signals by the North Eastern fireman, who was illegally driving the train alone in the absence of his driver.

Perhaps the hey-day of Carlisle's passenger traffic occurred in the first decade of the twentieth century. For instance, in August 1906 booked arrivals into Citadel over North Western metals alone between 1 a.m. and 6 a.m. numbered twenty passenger trains (remember this records only the arrivals of L.N.W.R. trains from the south). What a joyful all-night watch for the Edwardian railway enthusiast. Unusual evidence of the amount of night traffic and the warmth it created is supplied by the fact that pied wagtails roosted on the glass roof during the winter. These are one of the few species of birds which can adapt themselves to life on mountain-tops

9   One of the Problem class 2-2-2 singles which worked on the Lancaster and Carlisle Railway – No. 7 *Scorpion*, built at Crewe in 1859.

10 No. 39 *Thalaba*, Samson class 2–4–0, pilots a Black Prince 4–4–0 compound with an express from Euston in the 1890s.

11 Prince of Wales 4-6-2 Tank No. 1392 climbs away from Oxenholme with a local for Carlisle from Preston in 1924. The end coach is an L. & Y. six-wheeled brake and third.

and in towns. In those days very few of the trains would have been without a pilot engine; possibly three or four might have been Precursor- or Experiment-hauled but most must have been headed by one of Mr Webb's redoubtable four-cylinder compound 4–4–0s piloted by one of the little Jumbos.

In 1895 Carlisle became the terminus of the longest non-stop run made by the North Western up to that date, when the Webb compound *Ionic* made the journey from Euston with a special train of 150 tons. This feat was repeated in 1903 with an eleven-coach train which included nine twelve-wheeled diners, i.e. 450 tons; the motive power in this instance was provided by No. 1965 *Charles H. Mason* and No. 1966 *Commonwealth*. About this time two accidents occurred at Carlisle involving L.N.W.R. trains: both were due to a faulty automatic vacuum brake. In the second of these, on 4 March 1890, an express from the south composed of thirteen coaches and hauled by No. 515 *Niagara*, a Webb Dreadnought, ran right through the Station before colliding at the northern end with Caledonian light engine No. 62. Fortunately there were no serious injuries in either instance.

A consideration of the timing of North Western trains into Carlisle at the turn of the century may well be based on the 1888 Race-to-Scotland speeds, when the ninety miles from Preston to Carlisle was run in eighty-nine minutes by Newton class 2–4–0 No. 275 *Vulcan* with a train of four eight-wheelers, i.e. 80 tons. This was the 'best' time; the average during the races being ninety-six-and-a-half minutes. In contrast the time-table for normal working allowed 105 minutes for the non-stop 2.40 p.m. *ex* Preston. It should thus be noted that the Lancaster–Carlisle section

12 L.N.W.R. Experiment Goods 4–6–0 No. 8865 with an up coke train at Tebay, thirty-seven miles south of Carlisle.

13   A Preston–Carlisle semi-fast leaving Carnforth, headed by L.N.W.R. Precursor Tank,
with a very mixed rake of carriages.

was certainly smartly timed, and, in the opinion of many, remembering the difficulty
of the track, surpassed anything achieved anywhere else in the world. This
tradition was well maintained from 1900 to the end of the L.N.W.R.'s independent
life by, in turn, the un-superheated Precursors and Experiments, then the Georges
and Princes and finally the Claughtons with regular loads of between 350 and
400 tons.

Throughout its life in Carlisle as an independent company, the London and
North Western Railway lived up, in every sense, to the claim of its Euston manage-
ment, to be the Premier Line, and it paid the city the compliment of naming two
of its locomotives *City of Carlisle*; the first of these, built in 1885, was the 2–4–0
Dreadnought No. 3, and the second, a 4–6–0 Experiment No. 565 built at Crewe
in 1906. Later, the L.M.S.R. continued this tradition with No. 6238, a Stanier
Pacific.

14   The up Scotch Express leaving Citadel in charge of Prince of Wales 4-6-0 No. 2293
Percy Bysshe Shelley piloted by 4-6-2 Tank No. 1692, in the early 1920s.

15   An express for Carlisle leaving Lancaster in charge of L.N.W.R. No. 8, a 4-6-0 Claughton, in 1919.

16 A resplendent Experiment No. 1669 *City of Glasgow* poses for an official photograph at Citadel Station.

17 Two L.N.W.R. Jumbos in full flight! No. 1521 *Gladiator* pilots No. 1678 *Airey* with a
Carlisle to Manchester and Liverpool express over Tebay troughs in 1921.

18 Webb 2-4-0 No. 1531 *Cromwell* pilots Prince of Wales 4-6-0 No. 271 on an up express in Carlisle. The unusual leading coach is a composite first-class sleeper and third-class ordinary.

Chapter 2

The Caledonian Railway

The Caledonian main line from Carlisle to Beattock opened in September 1847 and the Beattock to Glasgow section was completed in February 1848, thus permitting the first through-service, with the L.N.W.R. from Euston to Glasgow, by the West Coast route. They were originally joint-owners of Citadel Station with the Lancaster and Carlisle Railway. Their line from Carlisle to Glasgow via Annandale is difficult, including as it does the ten miles up from Beattock and the second summit at Cobbinshaw; in fact the gradient is adverse for 34 of the 101 miles from Carlisle to Glasgow.

As any G.S.W.R. enthusiast would be quick to point out, the Caley was financed mainly from London, and its very name has been considered by some Scots to be an anonymous cloak to hide the real source of its monetary power. However, the staff obviously were almost all Scottish, and this may be considered a very minor debating point in the bitter rivalry which developed between the competing companies. Financially this was somewhat mollified when a traffic sharing agreement was made concerning the Carlisle–Glasgow routes in the late 1850s. The arguments at Carlisle, however, were of little importance compared to the bitter station disputes at Glasgow, before the Caledonian finally solved its problems there by building its own Central Station in the mid-1870s. This was obviously a great success when it is realised that arrivals and departures there were over half those of Waterloo or Victoria by the early 1890s. Some of these were, of course, from Carlisle, and one of the places where the Victorian and Edwardian engine-lover could best enjoy himself was the north end of one of the Border station's long platforms.

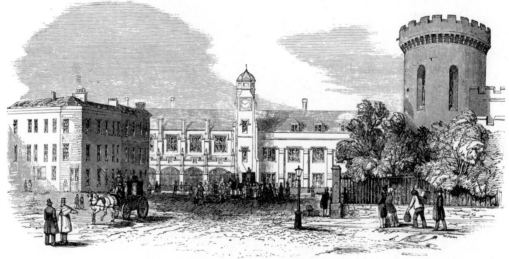

THE CENTRAL STATION, COURT-SQUARE, CARLISLE.

20 Perhaps the most famous Caley of them all! No. 123 piloted by the preserved G.N.S.R. 4-4-0 No. 49 at Kirkandrews-on-Eden on 13 June 1964 with an R.C.T.S. special.

21   C.R. Dunalastair class 1 No. 735 built at St Rollox in 1896 stands at the north end of Citadel Station.

Before 1923 the almost ritual change of engines always took place there at Citadel Station; for instance, in would come the train from Crewe, its fiery black slim-boilered monsters would uncouple, and the tired enginemen would gently shuffle them away, their fires now dull, their noble duty done! Then with that gentle squeal as it backed down, there would appear the large double-bogie tender of the Caley engine; one might hope for *Cardean*, but whether it was she or one of the Dunalastairs, one could be sure that she would be spotlessly clean and resplendent in that superb blue. (Apropos that blue: apocryphally it came about by accident in the 1890s, when the Caledonian painters 'thinned down' the sombre Prussian blue, then provided, with liberal doses of white lead, then freely available; they achieved such a pleasing result that it was adopted by the Board as the official livery!)

The Caledonian locomotives of these pre-1923 days were invariably spotless, their proud 'owners' were always polishing them and were seldom to be seen besmirching their work with an oil can; unlike their counterparts from Crewe and Upperby who seemed to perform these operations in reverse. Perhaps it was the least they could do in view of their reputation for thrashing them so mercilessly!

Certainly no more than a minute before departure-time, the Caley engine might commence to blow-off, and then with a short hoot from her whistle (which became familiar all over the United Kingdom after the L.M.S.R. took over) away she would go, her exhaust sharp and clearly defined as she headed confidently for her next stop, Carstairs.

Of all the world-famous Caley engines seen at Carlisle, perhaps pride of place should go to No. 123, the now preserved single wheeler. During the railway races of the late Victorian era, for instance, she left Carlisle with 150 tons on and then covered the 100 miles to Edinburgh at an average speed of 59 m.p.h., which of course included the ten-mile Beattock climb. Later in her life she was a regular visitor to Citadel when she was used as motive power for an engineer's inspection train.

The Caledonian rarely gave names to its engines, but one of those which it did name became a milestone in locomotive engineering. This was the giant 4-6-0 *Cardean* No. 903 built in 1906. Once her trials were completed she was seen daily at Carlisle for ten successive years, when she worked the 'Corridor', i.e. the 2 p.m. from Glasgow Central returning with the corresponding Euston train which left Citadel at 8.13 p.m. She was shedded at Polmadie and was regularly driven by David Gibson who was a well-known figure at Carlisle, especially to the boys who turned out in scores to 'see him off'; a kind of Geoff Boycott, to the boys of Headingley! It is perhaps a typical example of Derby's utter lack of any consideration for the traditions of her associates in the L.M.S.R. that *Cardean* was renumbered 14752 and that her historic number went to a compound, i.e. 903. Furthermore, in L.M.S.R. days *Cardean* ran namelessly. This engine was designed by Mr John F. McIntosh who

22 Caledonian 4-4-0 No. 927 leaves Carlisle with the Euston-Dundee express made up of L.N.W.R. stock, including a dining-car, and totalling 350 tons.

23   C.R. Dunalastair class 3 4–4–0 with an eight-wheel bogie tender awaits the 'right away' from Citadel Station.

24   C.R. 4–4–0 (L.M.S.R. No. 14450) stands outside Citadel Station with an empty stock train which includes a Pullman, second from the engine.

began his career as a fireman on the Scottish North Eastern and was eventually appointed Chief Locomotive Superintendent of the Caledonian in 1895. He had previously been responsible for the first of the famous Dunalastair 4–4–0s; these engines were really the precursors of the *Cardean* class which was simply an enlarged and improved six-coupled version of the original Dunalastair built in 1896.

Citadel saw the introduction of the first two Postal Expresses in 1885 when the Caledonian (Travelling Post Office) 'Day Down' and the L.N.W.R. (T.P.O.) 'Night Down' were inaugurated, each train carrying some thirty sorters. The only other train devoted exclusively to mail was the Great Western's Paddington to Penzance.

The Caley certainly had considerable influence on British railway policy generally and there are still many reminders of the one time presence of this great Scottish company at Carlisle.

25 C.R. 0–4–4 Tank, with a stove-pipe chimney, originally by J. F. McIntosh, and adopted by William Pickersgill, commences her ten-mile stint at the foot of Beattock; whilst the Moffat-bound connection leaves on the right.

26   A Caley '60' 4–6–0 approaches Gretna with a northbound cattle special in July 1950.

27   A general view of Viaduct yard looking northward from Carlisle No. 4 signal box.

Chapter 3

The Midland Railway

The Midland, the last company to reach Carlisle, only did so after sustained opposition from the West Coast monopoly; but eventually it was decided that they had to free themselves from the virtual stranglehold which the Euston partnership was then able to impose. They therefore began the supremely difficult task of constructing a completely new main line from Leeds, more than 100 miles northwards through the wild Westmorland mountains to Carlisle.

The route they eventually chose is undoubtedly one of the scenic wonders of the world's railways, and the Midland were not slow to exploit this when advertising their new service. Passenger traffic commenced on Monday, 1 May 1876, and from this date a third choice of route to and from Scotland became available. Midland metals proper end at Durranhill and the run into Citadel is over the N.E.R. which is joined at Petteril Bridge Junction for the short run into the joint station. The Dentonholme goods line leaves just before the L.N.W.R. main line is joined, and in olden days the Midland were left in little doubt of their inferior status as were their northern partners.

The Midland made no effort to mark the occasion with any special ceremony, but the local *Carlisle Express and Examiner* gave considerable space to inform its readers of the arrival of the new stately trains, with the beautiful Johnson engines, and Clayton's magnificent crimson carriages, with their seventeen coats of Derby paint.

A further point of interest was the burghers first opportunity to examine the massive American Pullman cars, with their covered-end platforms, which formed an

28   M.R. compound No. 1071 piloted by class 2 4–4–0 No. 412 leaving Citadel Station with an up express for St Pancras.

29 M.R. class 2 4-4-0s Nos 432 and 446 branch off the North Western main line with the morning Glasgow (St Enoch)–St Pancras express. An L.N.W.R. Experiment is in the background.

30 An up Theatrical Special with class 2 4–4–0 No. 463 piloted by 2–4–0 No. 228 (formerly No. 1478), built at Derby in 1880, stands in Citadel Station.

imposing part of the first Midland trains. Thus did the competition between the Midland and their old North Western rivals begin at Carlisle and in some odd way it has never ended, in spite of 1923 and 1948.

The new Midland route was almost eleven miles longer than that of its Euston rivals, i.e. 310 miles from St Pancras compared to $299\frac{1}{2}$ from Euston. There were many difficult geographical obstacles, Ais Gill (1151 ft.) being the most formidable, but in spite of all this the Derbymen were determined to obtain and to keep a large share of the Scottish traffic.

Six trains daily made the run from St Pancras to Carlisle, and two of these were through-expresses to Scotland. When Midland fares were set at 40s. 6d. from St Pancras Euston reacted, as might have been expected: the L.N.W.R. immediately reduced their fare from 47s. 0d. to 40s. 10d. Their journey time was one hour less than the newcomers and there was nothing the Midland could do about it; except what they did do, i.e. they offered superlative standards of comfort with their beautiful twelve-wheeled clerestory-roofed carriages, and they greatly extended the already very well-organised refreshment facilities provided at Normanton, where an excellent six-course meal was available during the twenty-minute halt at the station. Whatever the merits and demerits of the spirit of unbridled competition, it was certainly operating at full blast in late Victorian days. To quote an instance of this: how did the Midland's rivals make a profit out of the 6s. 0d. return excursion they ran to Windermere from Euston, for the skating during the severe winter of 1896–7?

During the initial years of their Scottish services, most of the M.R. locomotives

31 A Midland express stands in Citadel Station just after the amalgamation.

seen at Citadel were 2–4–0s of the 1302 series, but by the turn of the century the company realised that more powerful express engines had to be provided to take over from the small Johnson 4–4–0s which were by then the mainstay. Two completely new types of four-coupled locomotives were designed, and the first five of these were especially built for the Carlisle road. They were Nos 2606–2610 and had 6 ft. 9 in. coupled wheels and relatively large Belpaire boilers. They were also equipped with eight-wheeled bogie tenders. Their appearance at Citadel produced mixed feelings, for although they were quite handsome engines there was a nostalgic regret at the demise of the traditional Johnson grace. This can be compared with a similar view taken some twenty-five years later, in L.M.S.R. days, when the Royal Scots took over from the Claughtons on the Euston–Carlisle route.

Be that as it may, in the summer of 1902 one of the original compounds, No. 2632, was sent to Durranhill shed for trials on the Settle–Carlisle section and was later joined by No. 2631. The results were sensational, and apart from weight haulage some startling maximum speeds were recorded during the descent of Ribblesdale. The compounds were so successful that a further twenty-nine were built between 1905 and 1906 by Mr Deeley and, as is well known, the class was perpetuated by the L.M.S.R., after the hotly disputed trials with the L.N.W.R.'s Prince of Wales class 4–6–0.

The First World War saw the Midland services through Carlisle greatly disrupted by the endless stream of trains required to service Admiral Jellicoe's battle fleet at Scapa Flow. It was during the winter of 1918 that the only accident to happen near Carlisle involving a landslip occurred, and it says much to the credit of the original engineers of these difficult lines that this should be the only recorded instance of an

32   M.R. 2–4–0 No. 185 stands at the down platform in May 1936. Many of these long-lived
     Johnson engines received Belpaire fire-boxes and Ransbottom safety valves, thus
     dispensing with the once typical dome-salters.

accident from these causes. Deeley compound No. 1010 at the head of an eleven-coach train, the 8.50 a.m. *ex* St Pancras, entered Long Meg Cutting, twenty miles south of Carlisle, at 60 m.p.h., when a mass of clay slipped and covered the line ahead of her with hundreds of tons of earth. No. 1010 ploughed into this mass and was inevitably derailed. Seven people were killed and many injured. The Settle-Carlisle line was possibly the most treacherous in England and many additional retaining walls were built as potential dangers revealed themselves in the bitter winter weather. It was a dreadfully difficult line for the locomotive men and the M.R.'s notorious small-engine policy continued to demand the double heading of most of the expresses which crossed the Westmorland fells. The company, in spite of the spirited work of the compounds and the superheated 4–4–0s, never really caught up and it was not until after the 1923 amalgamations that the L.N.W.R. Claughtons and eventually the powerful Jubilees gave the Durranhill men the kind of motive power that they had so long deserved.

There is little doubt (with the benefit of hindsight) that the Midland's viciously applied economy drive, which was instigated in about 1907 and continued to the end of the company's independent life, bore heavily on the Settle–Carlisle section.

The operating staff, including the Carlisle footplate men, were left to cope as well as they could with many critical situations. But let us remember the Midland at Carlisle in its hey-day, with the Pullmans and the twelve-wheelers, the Johnsons, and the general air of unsurpassed comfort which the traveller enjoyed on this magnificent line.

33   M.R. No. 998 leaves the L.N.W.R. line with the up Scotch Express. This photograph gives some indication of the superb condition in which the Midland engines and carriages were maintained.

Chapter 4

The North British Railway

The North British opened in 1846 with the running of two special trains from Edinburgh to Berwick. The first ten years of operation were somewhat inglorious and its chief critics blamed all the difficulties on one major cause, i.e. English inefficiency. Rowbotham, the General Manager, was English, all the locomotives were built by Hawthorns of Newcastle, and the first three superintendents of the line also came from South of the Border.

The original ambition of the N.B.R. was to serve the South of Scotland, bordered by Edinburgh, Berwick and Carlisle, with their East Coast line as the base of the operation.

The Edinburgh–Hawick line was very expensive to construct, climbing as it did up the South Esk valley for eight miles at a 1-in-70 gradient, thence down to Galashiels and finally to Hawick; still forty-three miles from Carlisle.

The first engines to use this line were eight 2–4–0s built by Hawthorn (Nos 39–46) with 4 ft. 9 in. coupled wheels; fifteen more of this class were built by 1852 and

34   N.B.R. D 31 4–4–0 stands in the company's bay at the north end of Citadel Station.

35   The 1.15 p.m. local for Silloth leaves Carlisle hauled by N.B.R. 4-4-0 No. 36.

these were the last engines built by Hawthorns for the N.B.R. The extension from Hawick to Carlisle was bitterly opposed by the Caledonian who had their own plans for a single line branching eastwards from Gretna to Canonbie colliery, i.e. eight miles towards Hawick. This was, however, rejected by the House of Lords after being passed by the Commons, but after considerable legal wrangling the North British Railway was able to start work in September 1859 on the Carlisle extension, with permission to use Citadel Station when they got there!

Through three dreary winters the construction gangs battled with the difficult terrain, but after many civil engineering problems, including the collapse of the

36   N.B.R. 4-4-2 No. 878 *Hazldean* entering Citadel Station in the up direction with the up 'Diner'; the island platform was used for both up and down trains at this time (1919). This engine took part in the 1923 'Atlantic' trials between Newcastle and Edinburgh with North Eastern 'Z' class No. 735 and G.N.R. No. 1447.

north end of the Teviot viaduct, by September 1861 the southern section of the line was ready for operation and the line was opened, in stages.

Thus the first N.B.R. passenger service began out of Citadel Station on 28 October 1861 and it ran as far as Scotsdyke, fourteen miles north-east of Carlisle. The first train to run right through to Hawick left Citadel on 1 July 1862. It was fitting that the North British trains, passing as they did through the country made famous by Sir Walter Scott, should be time-tabled as 'The Waverley Route'. However, the line at this time never really functioned as the directors had intended; the L.N.W.R. and the Caley saw to that!

The Midland scheme to build an independent line from Settle to Carlisle offered the only hope of a satisfactory solution to the N.B.R.'s dearth of traffic. The through-service between St Pancras and Edinburgh began on 1 May 1876, and it is from this date that the Waverley Route may be said to have attained trunk-route status.

Although in 1876 the North British did not possess a locomotive suitable for express working over this difficult line, this lack of suitable motive power was quickly rectified by Mr Drummond with his excellent 4-4-0 express engines, the the first four of which (Nos 476–479) were named *Carlisle, Edinburgh, Melrose* and *Abbotsford*. They could run the ninety-eight miles from Carlisle to Edinburgh in 2 hrs. 10 mins. with the new Pullman trains, and their running became world famous. At the time, they were the largest and most powerful four-coupled engines in Britain and their only rivals were also Scottish, i.e. James Stirling's G.S.W.R. 4-4-0s of class 6. By the beginning of the twentieth century it was becoming quite clear that however diligently the N.B.R. maintained their part of the third way to Edinburgh, the service was unprofitable, and Derby was forced to sanction payments to the N.B.R. in settlement of losses incurred.

Dugald Drummond was succeeded at Cowlairs works by Matthew Holmes and the latter inherited a locomotive department well provided with express engines. His only design to penetrate regularly into Citadel Station was the 4-4-0 of the 729

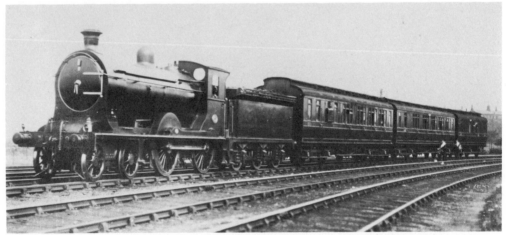

37   N.B.R. 4-4-0 No. 894 with the Waverley portion of the down Scotch Express from St Pancras.

38   0-6-0 No. 1875 waits to depart with the Langholm branch train in April 1946.

class, built in 1898. These 4–4–0s replaced the Drummond engines which had served nobly on the Waverley Route for more than twenty years, and were themselves long-lived engines, the last one to be scrapped being No. 768 in February 1951.

W. P. Reid succeeded Holmes, and in 1906 he produced a large Atlantic for use on the Waverley Route, since it was thought that the four-coupled engine would prove more successful on the sharp curves of the line than the then more conventional 4–6–0, e.g. Experiment, Cardean, Star, etc. These huge (for the time) locomotives were not an unqualified success; they were un-superheated and with loads of 250 tons and over they had to be piloted. No. 881 *Borderer* had a run over North Western metals in 1909 when the Premier Line allowed trials, with a special train of 290 tons, from Carlisle to Preston and back. The results were conclusively favourable to the

39   The various versions of the North British 'Scotts' and 'Glens' survived for many years after the 1923 amalgamation, and some into B.R. days. Here No. 62059 stands in Citadel Station with a Silloth branch train in April 1949.

40   N.B.R. 4-4-0 No. 2402 *Red Gauntlet* leaves for Newcastle with the 3.02 p.m. calling at Haltwhistle and Hexham.

41   A special train organised by Carr and Co. to take visitors to the re-opening of Silloth Mill, after its re-equipment in 1905.

42 L.N.E.R. No. 9876 *Waverley* decorated to take a works outing from Carr and Co. to the Newcastle Exhibition in 1929.

Experiment with which she was compared. No. 876 of the class was named *Waverley* and was regularly seen at Citadel. In 1909 came the famous Scott class 4–4–0s, the first being No. 895 *Rob Roy* and later the improved superheated edition with a 6 ft. variety called the Glen Class (1913). These engines were used all over the system, including the Waverley Route, and were well known at Carlisle. The last two express locomotives built for the N.B.R. by the North British Locomotive Co. were the superheated Atlantics No. 509 *Duke of Rothesay* and No. 510 *The Lord Provost* in 1919, by Mr Chalmers who had succeeded Mr Reid. He built two more of the class in 1921 and changed the locomotive livery to bronze-green.

Although it was a relatively junior partner in the Citadel consortium, the North British was a splendid railway which had its enthusiastic supporters in Carlisle; after all, it was the Scottish owner of the Port Carlisle Railway on the English side of the Solway Firth – an incursion which none of the other national companies ever achieved.

43　'Scott' class 4-4-0 No. 9499 *Wandering Willie* at Canal shed in 1930.

44　N.B.R. 0-6-2 Tank No. 69174 shunting in London Road goods yard. It was a long-lived little engine, designed by W. P. Reid in 1910 and seen here in July 1957.

Chapter 5

The Glasgow and South Western Railway

The Glasgow and South Western route from Glasgow via Dumfries reached Carlisle in 1850, after travelling over Caledonian metals from Gretna Junction into the city. In March 1851 the G.S.W.R. became a tenant at Citadel Station when it acquired a 999-year lease, and later in 1861 became a member of the Carlisle Citadel Station Joint Committee which was formed to ensure the better regulation of the Station.

From its very inception, the G.S.W.R. were bitter rivals of the Caledonian, whom they considered to be merely the tools of the English North Western. They had long cherished the idea of a line to Carlisle through the Burns country and down Nithsdale, which would be truly Scottish and controlled from Glasgow. Unfortunately this route had the perpetual disadvantage of being twenty miles longer than the Annandale line, but to compensate for this they were able to offer superior and more central facilities in Glasgow when they established themselves in 1876 at St Enoch's, after having previously terminated at Dunlop Street.

The first locomotive superintendent was Patrick Stirling, appointed in 1853, who was responsible for the famous singles of which the G.S.W.R. eventually had thirty-four. Later in 1873 James Stirling, younger brother of Patrick, designed his 7 ft. 1 in. 4-4-0s with a domeless boiler which coped ably with the Midland through-expresses which began three years later. They were most successful engines and twenty-two of the class were built.

45 A general view of Viaduct yard.

46   G.S.W.R. 2-4-0 No. 104 seen at Carlisle in 1895.

47   G.S.W.R. 4-4-0 No. 418 leaves Carlisle with the 6.40 p.m. for Glasgow, calling at Annan, Dumfries and Kilmarnock.

48   G.S.W.R. 4-4-0 No. 62 stands on the centre rail at the north end of Citadel Station.

When the St Pancras–St Enoch through-trains began in 1876, the drill at Citadel Station was relatively simple. On arrival from England, the complete train would be halted at the southern end of the long platform, and the Edinburgh section, i.e. the front portion, was uncoupled and drawn forward by the Midland engine which then returned light to Durranhill shed. The G.S.W.R. engine then backed on to the St Enoch section and the whole operation was completed in a few minutes. In those days the South Western engine was invariably a Stirling 4–4–0 of class 6 and these engines maintained the service until James Manson (1891–1912) took over from Mr Smellie (1877–91). They were long-lived engines and the last of them survived well into L.M.S.R. days. The G.S.W.R. shed at Carlisle, opened in 1896, was at Currock but it was closed down after the amalgamation. From the late 1870s the South Western engines had used Durranhill shed.

The 9.20 a.m. *ex* St Pancras through-train was known to all South Western railwaymen as the 'Pullman'. This always heavy train was seldom piloted out of Carlisle on its way northwards; the G.S.W.R. enjoyed a fairly easy run to Dumfries and it was not until there that they considered a second engine to be necessary for the climb up Nithsdale. This practice was interrupted when the 'Diner' from St Pancras to St Enoch was introduced in 1893; for the first time ever the stop at Dumfries was cut out and the 8 p.m. *ex* Citadel always had two Manson 4–4–0s, with special eight-wheeled tenders for the ninety-one-mile run non-stop to Kilmarnock. The 'Diner' was one of the casualties of the First World War for it was never reinstated after its cancellation as an economy measure. After 1918 the Manson 4–6–0s, introduced in 1903, which had to be worked gently because of their light framing, became less and less effective time-keepers, with the heavier trains they were required to cope with. Eventually, of course, came the L.M.S.R. and the common-user engines which worked right through from Glasgow to Leeds, when only the drivers and firemen changed.

So the Glasgow and South Western reached the end of its independence, and its association with Carlisle was submerged in the L.M.S.R. – gone are the days when

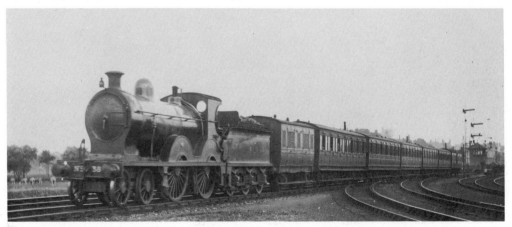

49 G.S.W.R. 4–4–0 No. 382 leaves Carlisle with the 10.38 a.m. semi-fast to Glasgow, due at St Enoch at 2.17 p.m.

50   A resplendent G.S.W.R. 4-4-0 No. 392 leaves Citadel Station with the 6.05 p.m. local to Dumfries.

the run into England was a great adventure for the South Western enginemen. Sadly the G.S.W.R. were the first of the pre-grouping companies to bear the brunt of the L.M.S.R. locomotive standardisation policies and their individualistic and much loved Mansons and Smellies were among the first 'visiting' Carlisle engines to disappear.

51   G.S.W.R. Peter Drummond superheated 4-4-0 No. 327 stands in the centre road facing north, with the N.E.R. bay in the right foreground and a waiting Claughton with her train in the background.

52 G.S.W.R. 4-6-0 No. 511 approaching Carlisle with the morning Scotch Express for St Pancras.

53   The railway siding entering the rear of Carr and Co.'s biscuit works in 1912.

Chapter 6

The North Eastern Railway

The Newcastle and Carlisle had the honour of providing a part of the first all-rail service from Carlisle to London (Euston) in September 1846 when it introduced its 8 a.m. train from London Road Station to Euston, via Gateshead and Rugby. It reached the capital at 9 p.m., i.e. in thirteen hours, and when the West Coast route opened some four months later, it took more than an hour longer over the journey!

The N.C.R. was also the first railway to be established in Carlisle – in 1836 – and reached the city through the various gaps where the Pennines end and the Cheviots begin. Its station was at London Road, which was also used at first by the Lancaster and Carlisle before it established itself at Citadel in 1847. The Newcastle and Carlisle did not achieve rail access to Citadel until 1849 and passenger access was not arranged until 1862 when the North Eastern took over the company. Prior to that, passengers travelling on from Carlisle had to make their own way from London Road to Citadel. When Citadel was enlarged in 1880 they had their own section of the station at the south-east end.

54   An interior view of Citadel Station in 1934.

By the late 1880s the N.E.R. had grown into the greatest and most important provincial railway; so much so that it developed designs on its southern neighbour, the G.N.R., in the hope of establishing itself in London. However, the nearest it ever came to this ambition was not achieved until almost fifty years later when railwaymen were apt to refer to the L.N.E.R. as the 'North Eastern'. The Newcastle and Carlisle was the most important branch in the northern part of the N.E.R. system and in the early 1880s most of the traffic was worked by the 5 ft. 6 in. engines of the '675' class. Three of these engines were shedded at Carlisle until the mid-1880s when the old Fletcher engines were replaced by McDonnell's '1492' class. All these engines built at Darlington were nick-named 'Quakers' because of the religious convictions of the leading developers of the old Stockton and Darlington. The '1492' class engines enjoyed a long spell on the Carlisle line until they were replaced by Wilson Worsdell's 4–4–0 7 ft. express engines on the faster trains. These were first-class locomotives and among the best ever to run on the N.E.R. into Carlisle.

Around the turn of the century, the North Eastern, in conjunction with the G.S.W.R., began a through-service of night expresses between Newcastle and Stranraer, connecting with the Larne cross-Channel steamers. The fastest journey ever time-tabled between Newcastle and Carlisle, i.e. sixty miles in ninety minutes, was thus introduced.

Also at this time, in collaboration with the Caledonian, through-carriages were

55   The North Eastern bay at Citadel Station.

56   N.E.R. 'Q' class 4–4–0 No. 1929 in the North Eastern bay. The locomotive was built at Gateshead in 1897.

57   The 10.14 a.m. Darlington train waiting to leave Penrith in April 1954. The cabs of these C1 0–6–0s appear to be much more roomy and well protected than their G.W.R. Dean, and North Western Cauliflower contemporaries.

attached to the 2 p.m. *ex* Central Station, Glasgow for Newcastle. These were, of course, detached at Citadel. With this 'train', the quickest journey from Glasgow to Newcastle was inaugurated.

The North Eastern was a fascinating line and contributed considerably to Carlisle's railway interest. Its immaculately maintained light green engines (beautifully outlined with olive green, black, vermilion and white bands, with oxide brown underframes also outlined with vermilion) were always a pleasure to behold, and though perhaps lacking the glamour of the continual bustle of the through-expresses of their neighbours, they provided a pleasant and colourful alternative for the onlooker at the Citadel railway scene. It is pleasing to remember that three of the N.E.R. Gateshead engines may still be seen in their preserved state at the famous Railway Museum at York.

58 Bridge No. 2 at Carlisle which carried the goods line from Upperby Junction to Crown Street, over the lines from Petterhill Bridge Junction to the N.E.R. bays and carriage sheds.

Chapter 7

The Maryport and Carlisle Railway

The first station of the Maryport and Carlisle was opened in 1843 at Bog Street, and when it moved into Citadel in 1852 it was of necessity the poor relation there. The line was only forty-two miles long, but it was truly independent, with its own engines and carriages, and its oldest section was opened in 1840. In its early days it had a vaguely Scottish ambience, perhaps mainly engendered by its locomotives which were designed by Hugh Smellie, who later replaced James Stirling on the Glasgow and South Western. In subsequent years it seemed that the North Western influence became paramount. The engines – there were thirty-three at the time of the company's absorption into the L.M.S.R. – were a rather unenterprising green, as were the carriages with their cream upper panels. They sported their own engine shed, which was near to Currock Junction, and their own goods station in Crown Street.

The Maryport and Carlisle was the southern end of the Solway Junction Railway, established in 1870, which ran from Kirtlebridge (C.R.) to Brayton (M.C.R.). It was built to bypass the congested traffic at Carlisle and crossed the Solway by a viaduct 1,940 yards long, second only in length to the Forth Bridge. In the winter of

59   The view south from the Maryport and Carlisle bay.

60   M. & C.R. No. 2 in the bay at Citadel Station.

1881 large floes of ice coming down-channel caused the collapse of forty-five of the 192 spans of the viaduct and although it was rebuilt during the next three years it was desperately expensive to maintain; in fact all traffic was suspended in 1921 because of its dangerous condition and it was finally dismantled in 1935.

The whole affair was pleasantly reminiscent of a very early Hornby outfit, but for all that, it added its share to the glorious panoply of railway miscellanea which Carlisle provided.

61   M. & C.R. 0–6–0 as L.M.S.R. No. 12080 stands at Maryport in April 1928.

62   The M. & C.R. line swings away to the west out of Carlisle.

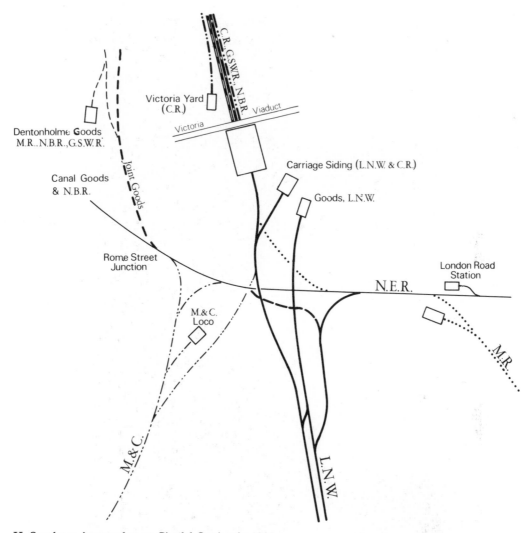

II Southern Approaches to Citadel Station in 1923

63   The Station forecourt in 1934.

Chapter 8

The London, Midland and Scottish Railway

The first new locomotive design to be seen at Citadel, consequent upon the formation of the L.M.S.R., were the Hughes 4–6–0s based on the pre-war Lancashire and Yorkshire express engine. They were painted in the new L.M.S.R. red and were employed with the Claughtons and Princes on the Crewe–Carlisle trains. A later Hughes design to become well known at Carlisle and particularly at Durranhill shed was his 2–6–0 mixed-traffic type, nicknamed 'Crabs', which filled a gap in the needs of the old G.S.W.R. They were considered by many to be rather ugly, but they did some fine work on passenger and goods trains. The first L.N.W.R. engine repainted in the new L.M.S.R. colours to be shedded at Carlisle in 1923 was Claughton No. 5971 *Croxteth*, and the first of the large reboilered engines of the same class to appear at Upperby in 1928 with the Royal Highlander was No. 5999 *Vindictive*.

Perhaps the most suspect locomotive innovations into the Carlisle district were the L.M.S.R.-built compounds. The North Western and Caley enginemen were quite happy with their Princes, Georges and Dunalastair IVs, which they thrashed merrily along, and the prospect of handling compounds was anathema to the Englishmen (remembering F.W.W.) and to the Scots alike, who knew nothing of them and did not want to learn, anyway. Nevertheless, the decision was out of their hands and gradually the newcomers came to be accepted for what they were, i.e. very good, modestly powered, reliable engines and they did some very useful work, particularly on the Scottish lines. The later class 2 L.M.S.R.-built 4–4–0s, with their limited power, were more readily accepted, and were to have many years of useful life in various capacities.

64   L.N.W.R. George V class 4–4–0 No. 5346 *Deerhound* pilots a class 5 4–6–0 with the Manchester–Glasgow express at Tebay in 1935.

65   The up platform in 1935.

However, in 1927 a class especially built for Euston–Carlisle expresses appeared, which was immediately accepted by the locomotive men, i.e. the Royal Scots built by the North British Locomotive Company. These, apart from the aforementioned Hughes engines, were the first really 'new' locomotive visitors to Carlisle since the amalgamations. There were fifty engines in the first series (Nos 6100–6149) and more were to follow, and they were all seen at Citadel.

The year before this (1926) Carlisle enjoyed a truly strange locomotive 'visitor'; from Swindon came No. 5000 *Launceston Castle* to undergo trials on the old North Western main line. Her performance there so impressed the Crewe examiners that the occasion may be considered as the seed which germinated into the appointment of the then Mr W. A. Stanier as Chief Mechanical Engineer of the L.M.S.R. in 1932. This was really the death-knell of the much loved, slim boilered, North Western stud of engines which had for so long maintained the Premier Line's reputation in its northern reaches. By 1943, in fact, there was only one Claughton left, No. 6004 *Princess Louise*, which was a rebuild with the large boiler, but she continued to be an occasional visitor from Crewe, usually with express parcels, until post-nationalisation days.

In 1933 Carlisle saw its first Pacific locomotive, *The Princess Royal*, and from that date onwards the principal Euston trains were hauled by Pacifics of various kinds. In 1937 came the arrival of the first of the streamlined trains when the 'Coronation Scot' was inaugurated, and during the same year the 'Royal Scot' express reverted to its previous habit of calling at Citadel instead of merely

66   L.N.W.R. Prince of Wales 4–6–2 T heads a semi-fast from Carlisle to Preston over Tebay troughs in 1933.

67 The down platform in 1935.

68 An odd combination! L.M.S.R. Patriot class 4–6–0 No. 45516 *The Beds. and Herts. Regiment* pilots a roller bearing class 5 4–6–0 No. 44762 with an express for St Pancras in July 1951.

69 Royal Scot class 4–6–0 No. 6106 *Gordon Highlander* approaches Carlisle with the Glasgow–Plymouth express; bearing Caledonian-type indicators.

changing engines at Kingmoor shed. This was useful for connecting North of England travellers and particularly so for the Carlisle residents who were thus able to reach London non-stop almost an hour quicker than previously.

The first streamlined trains seen at Carlisle revived memories of the Caledonian because of their blue casings, but later the L.M.S.R. had the last five of these trains painted in L.M.S.R. red, with gold bands. However, most engine enthusiasts preferred them uncovered anyway!

The company's publicity department had introduced the naming of certain trains which called at Carlisle; first of these was the 10 a.m. from Euston to Glasgow and Edinburgh which became the 'Royal Scot'. The train which all Carlisle railwaymen knew as the 'Corridor' became the 'Midday Scot' – but it continued to be called by their original name for it! The 'Night Sleeper' became the 'Royal Highlander' and even the Midland Scottish Expresses were boosted with titles such as the 'Thames–Forth' and the 'Thames–Clyde' – but to the railwaymen they always remained the 'Pullmans'. Carlisle must surely have been well to the top of any list of places served by 'named trains'.

Actually at this time the public relations men were enjoying a field day, and on 27 April 1928 the L.M.S.R., to pip their L.N.E.R. rivals who were planning a King's Cross to Waverley non-stop express, engaged in a publicity stunt to forestall their competitors. They ran a non-stop train from Euston to Princes Street, and it is not necessary to stress that it was a very light train, hauled by compound No. 1054, which became one of the few trains not to stop at Citadel. Whilst on the subject of long non-stop runs and remembering the L.N.W.R. efforts of 1895 and 1903

70   L.M.S.R. (*ex* Furness) 0-6-0 with an up coke train at Tebay.

71   L.N.W.R. Claughton 4-6-0 No. 5909 *Charles N. Lawrence* pilots Royal Scot 4-6-0
No. 6125 *3rd Carabinier* away from Carlisle with the up Glasgow–Manchester express
in 1930.

previously referred to, mention should be made of the non-stop trip on 26 September
1926 of the newly built No. 6100 'Royal Scot' from Euston to Citadel (299½ miles) at
an average speed of 52 m.p.h. with over 400 tons behind the tender. From October
1927 the 'Royal Scot' train was introduced non-stop between London and Carlisle
as a regular service.

The Midland Route was not neglected by the L.M.S.R., but perhaps its greatest
service was delayed until the introduction of the 4-6-0 Jubilee class engines in 1936.
The dreadful struggle up to Aisgill was surely banished into locomotive history when
No. 5660 *Rooke* on a test run climbed the forty-eight miles from Citadel to the
summit at an average speed of 60 m.p.h.

There were two serious accidents in the Carlisle area during the life of the
L.M.S.R. The first occurred in October 1928 when the down 'Royal Highlander' ran
into the rear of a stationary goods train at Dinwoodie. All four locomotive men of

72   Princess Royal class P7 Pacific No. 6203 *Princess Margaret Rose* nears Gretna Green
with a fourteen-coach express from Glasgow in March 1936.

73 February on Shap! L.M.S.R. XP5 No. 45500 *Patriot* reaches the summit with a Manchester–Carlisle express in 1960.

74 An unidentified Royal Scot picks up water at Tebay troughs.

75   Ex main line motive power at Keswick in 1930. L.N.W.R. 0-6-0 No. 8368 and Jumbo
2-4-0 No. 5034.

the express which was double-headed, i.e. a Dunalastair and an L.M.S.R. compound, regrettably lost their lives. The second accident occurred at Gretna Junction
when a goods train coming from the G.S.W.R. line and hauled by C.R. 4-6-0 No.
14650 was struck by the 10.05 a.m. Euston–Perth express in charge of compound
No. 1141. Three people were killed.

   After the war the L.M.S.R. gave Carlisle its first view of the shape of things to
come, with the introduction of the experimental separable double unit Co-Co diesels
Nos 10000 and 10001. Very soon after this, nationalisation took place and the
L.M.S.R.'s part in the Carlisle railway story therefore ended.

76   L.M.S.R. Stanier 2-8-0 crosses Denthead Viaduct on the Settle and Carlisle line with a
mixed goods on 30 May 1951.

Chapter 9

The London and North Eastern Railway

The Scottish constituents of the L.N.E.R. were much less affected in their locomotive policy than their compatriots who came under the L.M.S.R. Derby régime. These companies were the North British Railway and the Great North of Scotland. This brief look at the influence exercised on Carlisle is, of course, only concerned with the North British. South of the border, the North Eastern, as previously mentioned, would maintain that it was the L.N.E.R. anyway!

Sir Nigel Gresley, by training a Crewe man, who became Chief Mechanical Engineer of the L.N.E.R., always put great store on the care and maintenance of the pre-grouping engines he inherited, and consequently the North British retained much of its individuality in this respect for many years after, for instance, the G.S.W.R. had been submerged by its new and more powerful associates.

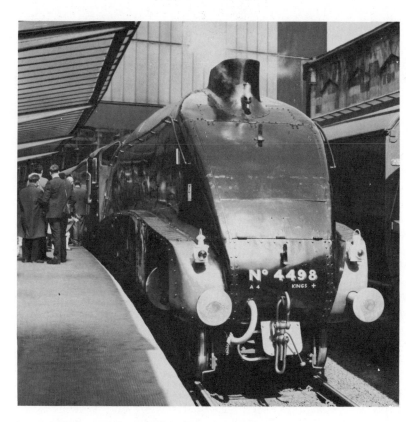

77   L.N.E.R. A4 No. 4498 *Sir Nigel Gresley* in steam for the B.R. open-day at Carlisle on 15 May 1970.

78   L.N.E.R. B1 3-6-0 No. 1100 leaves Citadel Station for Newcastle. To the left an
L.M.S.R. Patriot is backing down to her train.

However, whilst on the Waverley Route, with its many curves and severe
gradients, there could be no question of any startling cutting of times. Loads began
to demand some more powerful motive power and Gresley A3 Pacifics were introduced eventually and proved very suitable, although there was no opportunity for
any of the sustained speeds of which they were capable. But the L.N.E.R. were
aware of the qualities of their North British locomotive inheritance and the small-
wheeled variety of the Scotts, directly descended from the 'Waverleys' of 1876,
survived for many, many years, in fact into British Railways days.

Perhaps one of the most successful 'pukka' L.N.E.R. classes to tackle the
Waverley Route were the mixed-traffic 'Green Arrow' 2-6-2s, but the times from
Waverley to Citadel remained fairly constant; for instance, the 10.10 a.m. for St
Pancras calling at Galashiels, Melrose, St Boswells and Hawick was due in at
Carlisle at 12.49 p.m. and eventually reached London at 9 p.m. During 1960 and
1961 L.N.E.R. class 3 Pacifics worked some of the expresses between Leeds and

79 N.E.R. Worsdell 4–4–0 No. 1924 stands in the North Eastern bay whilst Midland compound No. 1022 waits on the centre line. One of the unusual features of the Worsdell 4–4–0s was the combined splasher which swept over both driving wheels. No. 1621 of this class is happily preserved with three other N.E.R. locomotives in the Railway Museum at York.

80 Hunt class three-cylinder 4–4–0 No. 364 *The Garth* leaves for Newcastle with the 1 p.m. express from Carlisle. These engines bore the names of famous hunting packs and carried a replica of a fox over the nameplate.

81 The 1.20 p.m. *ex* Carlisle due at Waverley at 4.10 p.m. halts at Riddings, fourteen miles north of Carlisle, in April 1953. This B1 class No. 61007 *Klipspringer* is one of the Antelope class of forty engines named after species of antelope.

82　L.N.E.R. V2 2–6–2 No. 60955 stands in Citadel Station with the Edinburgh–Sheffield express in August 1965.

83 An up goods from the Waverley Route at Rockcliffe, half a mile south of Floriston Crossing, hauled by A4 No. 60012 *Commonwealth of Australia*.

Carlisle, where their work was favourably compared to that of the Royal Scots. The A3s did on occasion work right through to Waverley. The Leeds–Midland shed drivers, who since 1948 had enjoyed a wide variety of engines for their most important turns, including Midland compounds, 999 simples and L.N.W.R. Claughtons, prior to the various Stanier types, were unanimously of the opinion that the Gresley engines were the best they had ever worked. The fastest train to Newcastle was the 3.02 p.m. *ex* Citadel which called at Haltwhistle and Hexham and reached Newcastle at 4.38 p.m. In the return direction the 2.20 p.m. *ex* Newcastle took exactly 1½ hours, although the night mail 12.20 a.m. *ex* Newcastle took only 1¼ hours non-stop. The Carlisle–Newcastle expresses in the years after 1935 were quite often hauled by three-cylinder Hunt class 4–4–0s which had the figure of a fox above the nameplate lettering. These were the D49s.

In the early 1950s Citadel saw some of its Glasgow–Crewe trains in charge of L.N.E.R. locomotives, when Polmadie shed became short of Pacifics and some A1s were temporarily transferred there from L.N.E.R. Haymarket. Because of this, Carlisle saw more of the L.N.E.R. Pacifics than any other station not on the North Eastern main line.

84   L.N.E.R. A4 Pacific No. 4498 *Sir Nigel Gresley* passes Durranhill Junction box, a typical M.R. box, with an A4 Society special to the Settle and Carlisle line in April 1967.

85   L.N.E.R. B1 class 4–6–0 No. 61221 leaves Carlisle with an express for Waverley in
     August 1952, while Princess Coronation class Pacific No. 66232 *Duchess of Montrose*
     waits on the adjoining line, where her fireman enjoys a hot water swill in his bucket
     before taking over the old 9.25 a.m. Crewe–Perth. The box is Carlisle No. 4, which (minus
     the semaphore signals) is still in use.

Certainly the L.N.E.R. 'carried the flag' very successfully into this stronghold of
its larger L.M.S.R. rivals and on one occasion in British Railways' days (28
October 1967) class A4 4–6–2 No. 4498 *Sir Nigel Gresley* made an astonishingly fast
run as a guest on the old L.N.W.R. line from Preston to Carlisle, completing the $88\frac{1}{2}$
miles in 97 minutes, thus knocking twenty-one minutes off the scheduled time.

However, such occasions have no place on present-day British Railways where
the accent is on the co-operation of the regions rather than on commercially senseless
competition.

86   An L.C.G.B. excursion hauled by Jubilee No. 45562 *Alberta* passes Durranhill box on the old North Eastern line on 3 June 1967.

87 An L.N.E.R. V2 No. 60957 on loan to Polmadie shed heads the Perth–London express over Mossband troughs in 1958.

88 London Road signal box with the spur to Upperby on the left, the goods lines leaving immediately after the box, and beyond them the siding of the Cowans Sheldon Crane Works.

Part Two

CARLISLE AFTER NATIONALISATION
(1948)

Chapter 10

Locomotive and Train Working

Any attempt at a brief résumé of the locomotive workings at Carlisle over the past twenty years or so is bedevilled by trying to separate the various classes of steam engine actually shedded at one of the four sheds there (Kingmoor, Upperby, Durranhill and Canal) and the others that passed through on their way to or from Scotland. In the early 1950s one of the features of the L.M.S.R. workings was the considerable number of through-workings off the L.N.W.R. section. The Liverpool and Manchester–Glasgow and Edinburgh trains worked with the same locomotives throughout, as of course did the Midland Route trains between Leeds and Glasgow. More surprising, however, in view of what must have been heavy maintenance arrears on engines after the war, was the large proportion of the London–Glasgow expresses that were not booked to change engines at Carlisle: this on trains that at the time frequently loaded to fifteen and sixteen total. Most of the heavier night trains did change engines at Carlisle. By the mid-1950s, however, the practice of changing engines on the day-time London–Glasgow trains at Carlisle had come back into vogue. In 1947–8 the up Royal Scot was not even booked to stop at Citadel, though in actual fact it stopped at Upperby to change crews. I have a vivid memory of this practice when on one occasion a man with a mound of luggage was decanted in Upperby yard by a very unfriendly ticket collector: having boarded the Scot in Glasgow under the impression that he was going to Motherwell! One Anglo/Scots train that always changed engines at Citadel was the St Pancras–Edinburgh service where the Leeds engines handed over to an L.N.E.R. Pacific for the journey over the Waverley Route.

Mention of the Waverley Route brings me to considering the workings of the ex-L.N.E.R. lines serving Carlisle. These duties were based on Canal shed and comprised, besides the Waverley Route traffic, turns to and from Newcastle and the Silloth Branch. When Canal shed was closed in the early 1960s, the ex-L.N.E.R. locomotives were transferred to Kingmoor but declined in numbers, as most through-workings from the north were based on out-and-back diagrams from St Margaret's shed in Edinburgh, and the line to Newcastle was one of the earliest in the North of England to be completely dieselised, again on an out-and-back roster from the Newcastle end. One or two of the various ex-L.N.E.R. 'J' classes were kept for Silloth for a surprisingly long time and as late as 1962 they had a virtual monopoly of the line. Considering all the radical changes that have come over British Railways in the last ten years, it is hard to realise that twelve years ago Carlisle boasted no less than four separate engine sheds, whereas now there is one; and, apart from maintenance, a relatively unimportant one at that. It has a horrible logic about it, in an era of rising prices and generally falling traffic, but this 'accountant's logic' is achieved at the cost of inflexibility and unreliability. Electrification may well restore

89   Duchess class 4-6-2 No. 46239 *City of Chester* at the head of the heavy up Midday Scot, passing Mossband box in 1958.

90 Duchess Pacific No. 46257 crosses the Esk Viaduct before the rebuilding; with the down
Royal Scot.

both, unless, of course, one of the great Westerly gales roaring out of the Solway
brings down the overheads across the 'Debateable Lands' of not so far distant
history.

To return to the late 1940s and early 1950s, each of Carlisle's sheds had a definite
function. Upperby was responsible for working the London trains and anything else
to the south over the old L.N.W.R. lines. As such it tended to have the cream of
Carlisle's express locomotives, mainly Duchesses and Jubilees. Its stud of 2-6-4
Tank engines also dealt with local trains to and from Penrith and Keswick, and most

of the steam workings to West Cumberland. The other shed to the south of Citadel was the old Midland shed at Durranhill, and as might be expected, this was responsible for all the Settle and Carlisle line trains, plus odd shunting services up the Eden Valley to various quarries and mines. But at this time it is not surprising that Durranhill was the poor relation of the Carlisle sheds, for the grouping of 1923 had reduced the frequency and importance of the Midland express services from England to Carlisle and the North. However, freight traffic over the high Pennines was, if anything, greater than over the L.N.W.R. and in its last years it was as a freight locomotive depôt that Durranhill earned its keep. Alas, the grouping under the Stanier régime, ultimately gave rise to a series of very efficient standardised locomotives on the L.M.S.R. and there was no point in keeping facilities for servicing the same types of locomotive at two separate sheds less than a mile apart. So, in the winter of 1959–60, Durranhill closed and the responsibility for working the Settle and Carlisle traffic went to Upperby. Of the two sheds to the north of Carlisle, the largest and most important was Kingmoor, originally built by the Caledonian and then, with the advent of the L.M.S.R., taking over the working of the G.S.W.R. trains when Currock shed was closed. I am told that there were some sore hearts and bloody noses for a few weeks then, for if there was one thing that the fiercely independent and deeply Presbyterian drivers of the South West hated more than the devil, it was the Caledonian, and to them the L.M.S.R. was merely the Caley in maroon livery. The last of the four Carlisle sheds in steam days was the Canal shed of the North British which by 1950 was servicing engines for the Newcastle road as well. This had a relatively sheltered life, if any shed round Carlisle could be said to have had such an existence. For just as a city which is set on a hill cannot be hidden, so the railways of a city set on an estuary surrounded by hills have to climb, and climb hard to get

91   L.N.W.R. Cauliflower No. 534 (L.M.S.R. No. 8476) at Keswick in 1929.

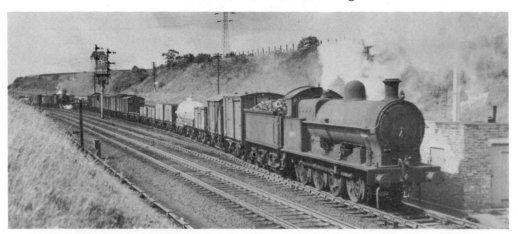

92   L.N.W.R. 0-8-0 No. 49190 joins the main line at Penrith with a Carlisle-bound goods
in July 1951.

out of it! The engines and men of Canal shed may have been relatively free of the
stresses of long distance Anglo/Scottish express working, but in the Waverley
Route to Edinburgh, and, to a lesser extent, the old Newcastle and Carlisle line to the
East Coast, they had very difficult routes to work. At least the Silloth line was flat –
which for a line in North West England was remarkable indeed.

So much for the Carlisle sheds and their functions. When it comes to the engines
shedded at them, the task of sorting things out twenty years ago becomes very difficult.
Upperby had the pick of the resident Pacifics – all of them Duchesses – for the
'Lizzies', as the L.N.W.R. men of this epoch called the Princess class, tended to live
on the southern division based on Camden or Crewe. It also had a stud of Scots, both
original and rebuilt: Patriots, mainly of the un-rebuilt kind, and Jubilees – the latter
always being popular engines with the Carlisle men as they could be thrashed up-hill.
Needless to say, a selection of Black 5s plus the odd L.N.W.R. 0-8-0 and Crab were
there, and even as late as 1952 some Webb Cauliflowers were kept for transfer-goods
working and for sending to Penrith for the Keswick line when the incumbents up
there broke down. Durranhill may have boasted the odd Jubilee plus a host of Class
5s, Crabs and 4Fs of Midland origin for the Settle and Carlisle workings. Canal's
allocation comprised three or four A3 Pacifics which were always kept in immaculate
condition for the Midland–Edinburgh trains over the Waverley Route, plus a fairly
large stud of V2s and B1s that worked to Edinburgh or Newcastle. Of the smaller
classes, there were some K3 Moguls and a selection of Js and a handful of 4-4-0s of
the Glen class. About this time there was also a Shire or two. The 4-4-0s worked
local trains to Hawick and out to Silloth.

Of all the Carlisle area sheds in the early 1950s, the hardest to classify was
Kingmoor as this was still very much responsible for the Scottish side of the border.
Undoubtedly it boasted a vast stud of Black 5s and the ubiquitous Crabs. In addition
there were several Caley classes, including a selection of Jumbos – the larger of
McIntosh's highly versatile 0-6-0 goods engines, plus some of the last series of
Caley 4-4-0s and a handful of Greybacks – the much abused but rather handsome

93   One of the ubiquitous class 5 4-6-0s No. 5583 approaches Gretna with a typical
L.M.S.R. express of the 1930 decade.

94   N.B.R. 4–4–0 class D33 No. 9866 at Canal shed, Carlisle.

Caley 60 class two-cylinder 4–6–0s. The Fowler epoch was represented in 4–4–0s, both of the P2 two-cylinder simples and the P4 compounds. Finally W.D.-built Austerities of both the 2–8–0 and 2–10–0 types were much in evidence. The 2–8–0s most certainly were heartily disliked. Other classes that worked from Carlisle consisted of the big Stanier/Fairburn 2–6–4 Ts plus a few of the older Fowler 2–6–4 Ts. A host of 'Jinties', one of which distinguished itself on a Glasgow Fair Saturday by hurling itself off the track at the south end of Citadel Station, and effectively blocking the whole up side for some hours.

In writing about the motive power of Carlisle in 1950, therefore, it is hard to say exactly where what was shedded because there was so much variety. Compounds and P2s came and went, and though the former tended to be concentrated on the Scottish lines plus a few on the Settle and Carlisle, most of these latter seemed to work in from Yorkshire rather than to be native. It would have been easier to list the L.M.S.R. classes that were not in evidence at this time and the most surprising omission in this category was the F8. Till the last three years of steam, these very efficient freight locomotives only got to Carlisle from other depôts in the South and to the very end none were ever shedded in Scotland. Other L.M.S.R. locomotives unknown in Carlisle were the 2–6–2 Tanks of either the Stanier or Fowler designs. Again it was the last few years of steam that produced this wheel arrangement in the form of Ivatt's 1947 design.

Turning to the train working, the immediate post-war pattern was maintained throughout the 1950s and with certain minor modifications right up to the end of steam. Taking the Anglo/Scottish services first; in the up direction the earliest departure from Citadel was a stopping-train from Carlisle to Crewe at 6.20 a.m. This was a strange train, made up of three or four coaches and a motley collection of vans: hauled by any power that Upperby happened to want to get back to Crewe – quite often a Pacific. In later days on summer Saturdays the motive power on this train became quite Somerset- and Dorset-like in its generosity. It once provided the very rare sight of double-heading Pacifics on the L.M.S.R. One July morning in 1963 it coasted down Shap with a Clan piloting a Duchess; this with four coaches and three vans made an interesting study!

The first through-train to London from Carlisle was the 8.40 a.m., again a Pacific turn which stopped at most stations as far as Lancaster, whereafter, picking up a portion from Barrow, it proceeded fairly swiftly to Euston. Before the southbound rush around midday, there was an early train from Glasgow to Liverpool and

95   L.M.S.R. Jubilee class 4-6-0 No. 45512 *Bunsen* heads a down Carlisle express near Preston Brook.

96 An Austerity No. 90145 with a stone train from Sandside to Tebay. These trains ran in connection with the construction of Kingmoor New Yard.

Manchester, normally a Jubilee working unless Polmadie was very well off for Scots. For Citadel the busiest part of the day in the up direction in the early 1850s came soon after midday beginning with the Royal Scot, Duchess-hauled from Glasgow to Euston. This was followed some twenty minutes later by the 10.05 a.m. Glasgow and Edinburgh to Birmingham, a train more often than not hauled by a Princess, but if one of these was not available, then by a Scot or Duchess. The third all-the-year-round train in the southbound procession from Carlisle was the morning Perth-Euston express which usually changed engines there. Upperby usually produced a Pacific but what brought it in was anyone's guess: it was seen with most things from a Duchess to a class 5 and on one occasion a V2! The last of the morning 'rush' from the North was the 10.40 a.m. Glasgow–Manchester, again a Scot or Jubilee working.

Carlisle, by its geographical position, has its peak traffic in concentrated bursts and if four West Coast expresses between noon and shortly after one o'clock was not enough, the two daylight expresses to St Pancras managed to get into the act around the same time. First of these to arrive was the 9.25 a.m. Glasgow (St Enoch) to St Pancras – named the 'Thames-Clyde Express' in 1950. This train connected with the Royal Scot and on many occasions, when all went well, they pulled out for the South together. Not for nothing had Leeds got hold of the first three or four rebuilt Scots, and one of the Holbeck ones – 6103, 6133 or less frequently 6107 – normally worked the Thames-Clyde run. Only when no Scot was available did an X5 have a turn on this train. The second train over the Settle and Carlisle in those far-off spacious days was the 10.10 a.m. Edinburgh (Waverley)–St Pancras which apart

97 An L.M.S.R. Hughes-Fowler 2-6-0 with a down goods at Mossband in 1958 before the addition of the second up line.

from serving Galashiels, Hawick, and some of the minor Border towns connected with the Perth–Euston and left Citadel soon after 1 p.m. About this time this train and its down counterpart were named the 'Waverley' – Walter Scott might well have approved, as of all the lines from London to Scotland, the scenery it traversed was the finest. An A3 Pacific brought it in from Edinburgh: *Coronach* or *Colorado*, one of Canal's, notably well-groomed for the immediate post-war epoch. What took it on was anybody's guess; with luck a Jubilee but often as not a Black 5 and in the summer very often a pilot as well. This working was to have a strange echo many years later when in 1966 and 1967 a through-train was run on Saturdays from Dundee to Blackpool via Edinburgh, and long after all else was diesel-hauled, a V2 would come in from the Waverley Route to be relieved by a Black 5 at Carlisle.

After the lunch-time rush, the up traffic fell off till the Midday Scot arrived shortly after 3 p.m. The 'Midday' was always a through-Pacific working from Glasgow to London and was followed shortly before 4 p.m. by the afternoon Perth–London which changed engines at Citadel and was worked forward by an Upperby

98 Carlisle Viaduct goods yard.

99 This train was part of an Enthusiasts trip worked to Carlisle by *Clun Castle*. While the *Castle* was being serviced, the train ran to Langholm and back, and is here seen passing through the birch woods at Floriston on the up goods line from Longtown Junction. This section was always quadruple track between the west end of Rockcliffe Station and Floriston level-crossing. When Kingmoor New Yard came into operation, the line was extended past Mossband to Longtown Junction on the N.B.R. for up traffic from the Waverley Route into Kingmoor New Yard. At the same time, it served the Ordnance sidings for the R.N. at Mossband. Cross-overs at Floriston enabled goods traffic from Gretna Junction to use it as well, but apart from excursions such as this, its use for passenger traffic was virtually unknown. The down goods line from K.N.Y. to Floriston is in the foreground and the two tracks in the middle are the passenger lines from Carlisle to Gretna.

100 Jubilee class 4–6–0 No. 45574 *India* and a class 5 light engine No. 45340 wait on the middle rails whilst No. 44903 stands at the head of a Glasgow–Morecambe holiday express in August 1965.

Pacific. At the height of summer, this was followed by a through-train from Glasgow to Liverpool. A further train from Glasgow and Edinburgh to Liverpool and Manchester left Carlisle shortly before 7 p.m. and ran all the year round. At the same time there was a train from St Enoch to Leeds over the Midland.

Tradition is a fundamental thing in railway operation and lives long. One of the great traditions of the West Coast Companys has been the intensity and variety of their night services between London and various parts of Scotland. These workings were so varied and complex that it would be too involved to go into them in detail, other than to say that Citadel around midnight must have been at its busiest in the up direction. Two trains are worth special mention. The first being that strange 7 p.m. from Glasgow Central that cast baleful glances at most of the larger stations from the Border to London and finally wandered into Euston shortly after 4 a.m. The other important Carlisle departure in the late evening was the up West Coast Postal which arrived in Carlisle between 9.30 p.m. and 10 p.m. and even in the war years continued to be a through-Pacific working between Crewe and Glasgow. The connections into this train were legion but the most interesting was probably the 5.30 p.m. *ex* Glasgow (St Enoch) whose claim to fame was the conveyance of a mail van and two through-coaches from Ayr to Carlisle attached at the back of the 5.30 at Kilmarnock – the mail van in those days going on to Newcastle, and for many years in a glorious vehicle lettered M. & G.N. joint stock. Now at certain times of the year this train was a through-service to Plymouth and was one of the earliest cases of regular Pacific working to Carlisle over the Nith Valley line. Indeed, it remained so till the end of steam, though in a very attenuated form.

The down passenger traffic also was worked to a long-standing pattern. The first arrival of the day was a stopping train from Warrington, which, in the last days of steam, was often a Duchess turn, but more usually a Jubilee or Black 5. This was followed around 11.30 a.m. by the morning train from Liverpool and Manchester to Glasgow and Edinburgh, which in the summer ran in two parts. Next to arrive at Citadel was the 10.25 a.m. Leeds–Glasgow, closely followed by the 9.25 a.m. Crewe–Perth. The Manchester and Leeds trains were through-workings, usually with a Jubilee or sometimes, if the Motive Power boys were feeling very generous, a Scot. The Crewe–Perth changed engines in Carlisle and this train seemed to be worked on the principle of anything worked it in and anything worked it out, though in the early 1950s the un-rebuilt Patriots predominated between Crewe and Carlisle. There was then a long gap until about 4 p.m. when the down Royal Scot, the Birming-ham–Glasgow and Edinburgh, and the Euston–Perth followed one another into Citadel in bright array. The first two were through-Pacific workings as a rule, with a Duchess on the Scot, and a Lizzie (Princess) on the Birmingham. (Upperby were always strict on their aristocratic titles and to them a Princess was always a 'Lizzie' and a Duchess a 'Big Lizzie' : what *Burke's Peerage* would have said about this is best left un-mentioned!) Also between 4 p.m. and 5 p.m. the two principal Midland expresses of the day came off the Settle and Carlisle – the 'Thames–Clyde' Scot-hauled and the 'Waverley' (though this title came later), normally worked by a Holbeck Jubilee to be taken on by a Canal A3.

In high summer, an afternoon Liverpool–Glasgow and a Birmingham–Edinburgh managed to work into this early evening rush, but normally the next train of any note was the 'Aberdeen'. This was a classic case of wrong naming. In actual fact the train was the 10.40 a.m. semi-fast from Euston to Carlisle! Again more often than not a Duchess turn. Finally in a minor rush between 7 p.m. and 8 p.m. the Midday Scot from London, the 4.30 p.m. Liverpool and Manchester–Glasgow, and the London–Perth arrived. The Manchester train was as usual a through-working for a Jubilee or Scot but both the London trains changed engines in Carlisle. The Midday exchanged Pacifics, and the Perth which started with a Pacific was relieved by a Jubilee. In addition there was an interesting working over the G.S.W.R. at 7.50 p.m. (latterly 7.40 p.m.) connecting with the various trains from the South. This train was semi-fast to Glasgow (St Enoch) and was very often a Pacific working. A similar connection went out over the Waverley Route with a B1 or V2. However, in the tradition of West Coast workings, much of the traffic went through Carlisle by night, but on these trains locomotive changing was the general rule on account of the heavier loads conveyed.

The day-time workings through Carlisle remained virtually the same till the introduction of the electric/diesel-hauled services in 1970. The only exceptions were the introduction of an early morning and evening Caledonian service between London and Glasgow in both directions in 1960. These trains were originally of light formation and at the outset Pacific-hauled throughout, but once the electrification of the lines south of Crewe got under way, the Pacifics worked between Crewe and Glasgow only, and south of Crewe the working became mainly diesel, with a little electric power as various sections became live! By 1961 the Caledonian workings were all diesel-hauled by the English Electric class 40s, as were many of the through London–Glasgow services. But most of the intermediate services were still in the hands of steam. By 1962 the writing was definitely on the wall for steam-hauled Anglo/Scottish trains as more and more diesels took over. The last to be steam-hauled were the Liverpool–Glasgow trains and some of the London–Perth ones. However, by 1963, other than in emergencies, all the West Coast regular passenger trains were diesel-hauled. Summer Saturday reliefs were a different story and steam remained on them till 1967, at least south of Carlisle – in some cases steam was still in use in the early months of 1968. The Midland Route showed a similar pattern, though in 1967 two of Holbecks Jubilees, *Kohlapur* and *Alberta*, staged a swan-song which earned them immortality, by working reliefs to the down morning Leeds and the down Thames–Clyde Saturday after Saturday – these were stirring times!

The train and locomotive workings of the 1950s set the pattern till 1970, and one of the strangest features about this was that the replacement of steam by diesel engines altered neither the pattern of the trains nor the timings to any great extent. The first major alterations of half a century came in 1970 with the introduction of class 50 diesels working in multiple: but this is in the future. Between 1950 and 1970 while the general pattern of train-working altered very little, there were considerable changes in the motive power available. The standardisation of L.M.S.R. motive power brought about by Sir William Stanier resulted in the main lines to

101 A view from the footplate of No. 45562 *Alberta* as she enters Citadel Station with a Saturday Thames–Forth express in August 1967.

102 Type 4 Diesel stands at Citadel Station's main platform for the North with a Leeds–Glasgow express on 19 August 1967.

103 A Glasgow–Blackpool holiday relief stands at the up platform whilst Britannia No. 70010 waits on the down line in 1965.

the North through Carlisle being little touched by British Railways standard locomotives for a long time. This was especially true of the Scottish services, where as late as 1952 goods trains were being worked by the Caley class 60 4-6-0s. In 1951 some abortive trials were made with Britannia No. 70016 *Ariel* over the Midland Route from Leeds to Glasgow. These were so ineffective that the Britannias got a bad name at Carlisle which they never lived down – in the best traditions of Border rail-roading they were christened the 'Gutless Wonders' and with some justification, for of all the many classes of steam locomotive to pass through Citadel they were probably the worst. Enginemen's prejudice partly, but it was all too often borne out by personal observation – they wouldn't climb and couldn't be thrashed, and if there were two features that locomotives working from any of the Carlisle sheds had to have, it was the ability to climb and be thrashed in good measure! By early 1952 the first standard class to work regularly through Citadel was the Clans, taking turn about with the Scots and Jubilees on the Manchester–Glasgow jobs. On these trains they did rather well: indeed there are good reasons for thinking that the Clans may well join the Webb compounds as being the most unjustly maligned of all West Coast locomotives. Not for nothing were the last five Clans shedded at Kingmoor, and in regular use at that: while a large stud of Britannias were left in the back row – hoping that no foreman might confuse bulk with efficiency! With the exception of the Clans, the standard locomotives were little in evidence at Carlisle till 1961, and by then diesels were beginning to come into evidence. All through the 1950s the well-proved L.M.S.R. classes handled the bulk of the traffic: Duchesses and Lizzies, rebuilt Scots and Jubilees. The original Patriots fought a gallant rear-guard action over the fells but seldom penetrated into Scotland – their rebuilt versions held sway till the end of steam.

I have mentioned the glamour locomotives, but all around Carlisle for twenty years after nationalisation the Black 5s filled the role of all-purpose workhorse. Now that steam has gone, the class 5s of the L.M.S.R. stand as the greatest British design of that fascinating century. And nowhere more than round Carlisle. They did everything, and by their very efficiency a host of smaller, older and less efficient classes went to the wall. The compounds were the first casualties, followed rather rapidly by the Caley 4-4-0s, the Greybacks and, after a remarkably long struggle, the L.M.S.R. P2s which survived as pilots over the Settle and Carlisle till 1961. While the older orders of pre-grouping locomotives changed, the new ones which replaced them were proven L.M.S.R. types. The big Ivatt Moguls came to stay, the delightful 'Mickey Mice' . . . the Ivatt class 2 Moguls came to Upperby to work the Keswick Branch and overflowed to all sorts of light duties. Belatedly in the early 1960s Kingmoor acquired a stud of 8Fs. It was only in the mid-1960s that the standard British Railways classes came to make their mark: Kingmoor acquired a stud of Britannias which it shared with Upperby (and were equally disliked there). The standard 5s were never shedded at Carlisle although the 76XX Moguls worked in from Scottish depôts such as Ayr or Hawick. The most successful of the B.R. classes to come to Carlisle were the 9Fs and these were used by Kingmoor on nearly every line it served – they even got some good work out of the modified Crosti ones, which must have taken some doing! Strange to say, one of the last classes to be

104 This train is climbing on to the new bridge over the up and down Caley lines and the goods lines into Kingmoor New Yard. Just off the left of the picture are the run-round loops at Stainton where locos that had worked out goods trains from K.N.Y. for the Waverley Route ran round their trains before setting out for the North. The particular line that the train is on is still used as far as Brunthill sidings for R.A.F. traffic, and thus indirectly is the only part of the Waverley Route still in existence.

105 B.R. Britannia Pacific No. 70021 passes Bog Junction box with a northbound goods from Leeds in November 1967.

106 Class 8F 2-8-0 No. 48151 with a southbound Goods. The train is actually pulling out of the departure section of K.N.Y., the lines to the arrival side are seen on the left. The two lines on the right are the old Caley main lines to the North. The new Kingmoor signal box is out of sight on the left.

shedded at Carlisle was an Ivatt design, the 2–6–2 T. With the closure of the Somerset and Dorset, some of these came to replace the Jinties at Citadel on pilot duties and for running short passenger turns, such as the workers train to Harker.

Before considering the full dieselisation of the northern sections of the L.M.S.R., we must look at the workings on the ex-L.N.E.R. lines. These varied little in the 1950s and by early 1960 were nearly all dieselised. Till 1961 A 3s and V 2s virtually monopolised the Waverley Route traffic. B 1s worked Carlisle's turns to Newcastle and the reciprocal jobs brought anything that Gateshead had to spare, from A 4s downwards. Various 0–6–0s attended to the Silloth Line, though after the ex-L.N.E.R. locomotives had been transferred to Kingmoor, the big Ivatt Moguls came into evidence on this line. The first serious effect of dieselisation was seen on these ex-L.N.E.R. lines and by 1961 virtually all passenger trains over the Waverley Route were diesel-hauled and those to Newcastle were D.M.U.s. Freight working to and from Edinburgh proved some of the last and hardest tasks for Haymarket and St Margarets Pacifics of the A 3 and A 1 classes, with Kingmoor laying on Black 5s and the occasional 9 F from the southern end.

On the ex-L.M.S.R. lines the advent of diesels came slowly at first, with some of the through London–Glasgow trains being dieselised with E.E. class 40s as early as 1961. The Birmingham–Glasgow turns followed the next year and by the summer of 1963 all the main expresses from Glasgow to the South were diesel-hauled. Three years later extras and summer reliefs were still worked by steam and it was only in the summer of 1967 that steam on summer-holiday trains became the exception rather than the rule. By this time Black 5s and Britannias were in the ascendant and

107 Northbound train on the goods lines at Dentonholme North Junction. The junction box is in the fork of the tracks. The lines on the right go into Dentonholme yard (just visible in the centre background) with the yard shunter sitting on the down line. This is now the only goods yard serving Carlisle city.

108 In 1950 four L.T.S.R. 4–4–2 Tanks were sent to Carlisle for local duties, but they were unpopular and were soon set aside. Three of them are seen at Durranhill in June 1951.

on certain trains, such as the Glasgow–Morecambes, on summer Saturdays the Scottish Region worked in with a diesel to have a steam engine work on. This same summer of 1967 saw the swan-song of the Jubilees over the S. & C.R. Also in 1967 the class 47 diesels took over from the class 40s as the mainstay of West Coast express working, with the inevitable Peak class on the Midland Route trains. Freight traffic was worked by anything that happened to be available. And so the pattern remained till 1970. The trains and their timings were virtually the same as L.M.S.R., or for that matter L.N.W.R. days. Certainly the summer Saturday extras were fewer, and the days when trains from the North on Glasgow Fair Saturday were stacked up block to block back to Kirtlebridge, and anything which had no reason to stop at Citadel was sent by the 'goods lines' had gone. But as late as 1967 there were still peaks of great passenger activity in the Carlisle area. The end of 1969 and early 1970 were years of peace, with class 47s working the principal expresses, and class 40s on most of the extras.

The late 1960s saw the arrival on the West Coast lines of the English Electric class 50s, on paper and in practice no more powerful than the Brush-built class 47s, but they did have the most sophisticated control gear of any British diesel, a fact which in their initial months caused quite a lot of trouble. This made it possible to work them in multiple, or singly, as the occasion demanded, with very little trouble. This fact, coupled with considerable improvements to the track and curves of the Crewe–Carlisle main line and to a lesser extent in Scotland, brought about a revolution in Anglo/Scottish services on the old L.M.S.R. lines. With the closing of all stations between Lancaster and Carlisle, except for Carnforth, Oxenholme and Penrith, there was no need for stopping trains and even 'Lulu' disappeared. (Lulu being the

109 A most unusual sight at Citadel Station; a non-passenger train passes through, i.e. a Broughton–Maiden Lane meat special hauled by No. 46241 *City of Edinburgh*.

110 A rebuilt Scot No. 46107 *Argyll and Sutherland Highlander* with a Carlisle–Glasgow express waits alongside Type 2 Diesel No. 530 with a Carlisle–Edinburgh train.

early Warrington–Carlisle which had the reporting number 1L00 – hence the typical irreverent nickname!) Instead, the basic idea of an hourly service from London to Carlisle at 0.05 minutes past each hour between 8 a.m. and 4 p.m. was introduced. The trains leaving Euston at five minutes past the even hours were the through London–Glasgow workings, while those after the odd hours went to Carlisle only, but were run as full trains to Preston with the rear parts going on from there to Blackpool, Barrow or Windermere. Needless to say, everything was electric-hauled south of Crewe. North of there, the general rule was that Glasgow trains rated two class 50s working in multiple, whereas those only going as far as the Border boasted only one. There were exceptions to this, for example the 11.05 a.m. *ex* Euston only ran a Carlisle portion on summer Saturdays, while the 3.05 p.m. was a Blackpool train pure and simple. But by way of compensation, Carlisle had a 6.05 p.m. from Euston. In addition there was a 9.25 a.m. Crewe–Carlisle connecting out of the 7 a.m. Euston–Manchester. These intermediate trains served all the stations remaining open north of Preston. The night trains, however, stayed to the pattern of the previous half-century, though there was an extra one to and from Glasgow by the G.S.W.R. route and the number of sleeping cars conveyed was increased.

In the up direction, a similar pattern evolved, giving nearly an hourly service from Carlisle but with departure times not nearly as evenly spaced as those from Euston. A surprising omission in the first year of this new schedule was the lack of an early train from Carlisle to the South, as the old 8.40 a.m. had gone and passengers were supposed to try and squeeze into the often overcrowded 7.40 a.m. *ex* Glasgow. In the 1971 time-table this has been remedied by a 6.55 a.m. Carlisle–Euston serving most of the main stations in North West England and still arriving in London four minutes after midday.

The re-casting of the provincial expresses was even more drastic, if not as logical. The mid-morning Glasgow–Birmingham services vanished except for during a few weeks in summer, and a train blighted by the fatuous name 'Midland Scot' left Birmingham for Glasgow at 8.15 a.m. calling at Carlisle at 11.49 a.m. This train conveyed a portion for Edinburgh, and returned in the evening, leaving Glasgow at 5.30 p.m. and arriving at Carlisle at 7.18 p.m. The Glasgow–Liverpool workings remained virtually the same, though the down morning train and the up evening one rated two class 50s in multiple, though the corresponding trains did not. Owing to electrification work in 1971, these trains have had their timings slightly increased to allow for running over the Nith Valley line in Scotland and for certain unavoidable checks on the L.N.W.R. Potentially they represent a very good service, but in practice, snags have arisen through too intensive rostering of coaching stock; any trouble with the stock in the morning tends to have a serious snowballing effect on running for the rest of the day. In fairness, however, it must be admitted that these trains are clearly a try-out for the shape of things to come with full electrification.

If variety is lacking in 1971 in the passenger workings through Carlisle, it certainly is not with freight traffic. The bulk of the freight traffic from the South is handled by the E.E. class 40s and the Derby–Sulzer 'Peak' class. Onwards to Scotland the E.E. Type 3s predominate with a scattering of class 2s of various makes

111 A visitor to the Settle and Carlisle G.W.R. 4–6–0 No. 7029 *Clun Castle* passes Durranhill
Junction box with a L.C.G.B. special on 14 October 1967. *Clun Castle* is now the property
of a preservation society and is regularly on view at Tyseley G.W.R. shed in Birmingham.
See also plate 99.

112 A dismal scene of stored locomotives at Upperby M.P.D. At this time Upperby still had a few
steam engines based there mainly for local freight working. On 1 January 1968 it closed for all
except D.M.U. maintenance but the stored/condemned locomotives stayed on for a few more
months. All diesel maintenance was transferred to the new diesel depôt at Kingmoor towards
the end of 1968, but the yards are to be used for stabling trains in connection with West Coast
electrification work.

and shapes. On the Newcastle and Carlisle line again E.E. Type 3s are in the majority. Local workings are liable to turn up most things from Type 1s upwards, though the advent of the Clayton–Paxman Type 1s from the Scottish Region was short lived and left a nasty taste in the mouths of the Carlisle men. If the motive power on freight trains is varied, the routing of such trains is less so, for with the advent of the new West Coast passenger services in May 1970, freight traffic was all but banished from the great main line over Shap. Freight liners with the inevitable class 47s still go this way, plus some parcel trains: but apart from the limestone trains from Hardendale (Shap Quarry) on the north side, and various block trains from the granite quarries at Shap Summit on the south, there is now no through-freight working over the old L.N.W.R. main line. It all goes by the Settle and Carlisle line – the West Coast traffic going west at Hellifield through Blackburn and back to South Lancashire or Crewe, while that for Yorkshire and the Midlands goes on through Skipton. The Settle and Carlisle can never have been as busy in its life, but this blaze of glory may well be its last; for with electrification it is marked for closure, at least between Appleby and Settle Junction.

The past twenty years have seen great changes in the railways of Carlisle, both structurally and in the motive power field. Kingmoor New Yard has come and the Waverley Route gone. Diesels growl where once the Greybacks spluttered, the mighty Duchesses passed out in their prime, replaced by class 40 diesels at the stroke of an accountant's pen. The Stanier 5s came, proliferated and conquered, then vanished into limbo as class 47s stood in their place. Britannias came, were cursed and died: the 9Fs came too late, but made a very favourable mark. Only in Lancashire did steam survive longer than at Carlisle, but, as I write, steam has the last laugh; for while steam served Citadel for 120 years in all its endless variety, the diesel epoch will be lucky to last twenty – its variety a poor thing by comparison with the endless steam pageant from Bloomers to Britannias. Yet, as in steam days, Carlisle has seen more variety of diesel power than most places. What electrics may bring is in the future, but one thing is sure: for as long as there are railways, the strategic position of Carlisle will ensure that it is one of the key railway centres of the United Kingdom.

Chapter 11

Civil Engineering and Signalling

From the fog of war and the darkness of the black-out, tales of railway working round Carlisle emerge like ghosts from an unopened cupboard in a long untenanted castle. There is one I can authenticate, and which is worth the telling, if only to give an idea of just how busy a railway centre the Border City was during these six strained years. A fireman and his mate were booked on at Upperby to relieve the crew of a northbound freight, and duly walked the few hundred yards to Bog Junction signal box (now Carlisle No. 10 and soon to vanish under the new signalling system). They climbed on the footplate and relieved a crew who had worked off the Midland. Seven hours later they climbed off again and walked back to Upperby for their train had got no farther than Canal Junction! Two miles in seven hours was poor going, even by the congested standards of Carlisle in 1944, but it was not unique. What was unique was Carlisle's geographical position: it was the heart of the arteries that circulated the greatest proportion of traffic between Scotland and the northern half of England – the only other point of contact of importance was Berwick. But by the laws of geology most of our industrial output is concentrated on the west side of Britain,

113 Long-lived North Western signals against the wall of Citadel Station.

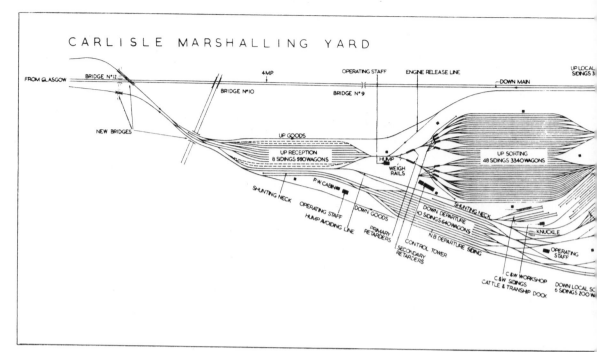

114 Plan of Kingmoor New Yard.

so Carlisle became the all-important bottle-neck for freight traffic. Strange to say, Carlisle never generated much freight traffic on its own – it made biscuits and some very efficient but specialised cranes: no, its main importance during the last war and for several centuries before, was as a communications centre. The importance of the fortified castle to stop the Scots raiding the Cumbrian cattle, or come to that to protect the Cumbrians returning the compliment, was carried in a different way, into the Railway Age. Not for nothing did Carlisle become the mecca of seven, or eight if you count the Furness, different companies. We would call it a communications centre today and for once modern jargon would be reasonably accurate.

Part of the art of communication is speed and convenience, and clearly anything that takes longer on the last three miles than on the initial 130 is inefficient. Thus every alteration that has been made to the railways about Carlisle since nationalisation has had but one aim, namely to speed the interchange of freight between Northern England and Western England with South and Central Scotland: passengers were also considered, but to a lesser extent, since by the 1950s the number of passenger trains handled, even at peak periods, was a poor thing compared with say the first decade of this century. Carlisle was lucky in one respect, the pre-grouping companies opened an elaborate system of avoiding lines for goods traffic on 7 August 1877. What they had not been able to agree about was a combined marshalling yard, thus eliminating various 'cross-town' shunting movements, all of which added to congestion. In the days of seven or eight rival companies this is understandable, but had the L.M.S.R. and L.N.E.R. shown as much enthusiasm for simplifying their freight interchange at Carlisle as they did for a combined locomotive testing plant at

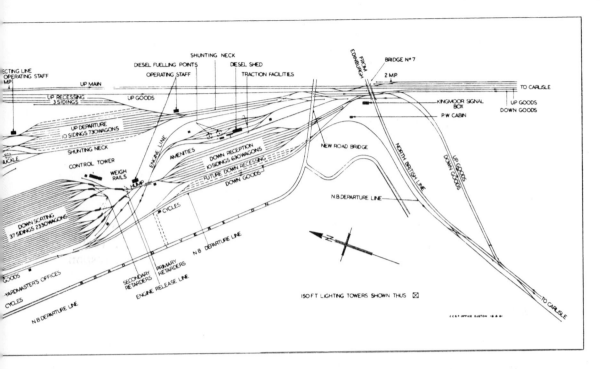

Rugby, life for all at Carlisle during the Second World War might have been a good deal easier. British Railways saw the need for this and did it splendidly with the new yard at Kingmoor, but alas even their vision did not go far enough and see this as a means of eliminating expensive marshalling facilities in Scotland into the bargain. The main alteration to train-working round Carlisle since 1948 has centred on Kingmoor New Yard, so much of this chapter has to deal with this re-organisation.

The story of the construction of Kingmoor New Yard and the consequent alterations to track and signalling belongs to the early 1960s, so before considering this it is necessary to mention various alterations to the passenger workings round Citadel Station. The first of these was the replacement of two vintage L.N.W.R. signal boxes at the south end of the Station. The more important of these, the old No. 5 box, was situated on the east side of the line immediately beyond the Station. The other was Carlisle No. 6 box, set in the junction of the L.N.W.R. and Maryport lines, 150 yards south of Citadel. Both these boxes were replaced by the new No. 5 on the west side of the lines, fifty yards from the platform end. For its day this was a very modern power box but it has been fated to a short life as a new power box is now being constructed behind No. 5 to control the Carnforth-Kirkpatrick lines, once the West Coast electrification to Glasgow is complete. There is some doubt as to when the 'new' No. 5 box actually came into operation, the official date was, however, March 1953. Concurrent with the opening of the 'new' No. 5 box, all the semaphore signals in the Station area were replaced by coloured lights. The other alteration to Citadel in the 1950s was the removal in 1958 of the very impressive overall roof of the Station from all but the central section, and even this was considerably modified to give better illumination. However, when this roof was removed, the walls that supported it were allowed to remain, though now with no function other than wind breaks against the gales sweeping in off the Solway or down from the high fells.

By the end of the 1950s it was becoming obvious that both goods and passenger traffic on the railways was declining and changing in nature, and one of the results of this was the closing of the Durranhill engine sheds in the winter of 1959–60. Durranhill shed had been the Midlands shed in pre-grouping days; the responsibility of providing power for the Settle and Carlisle line was transferred to the ex-L.N.W.R. shed at Upperby and then in the final hours of steam to Kingmoor. However, the old Midland goods yard at Durranhill remained in existence till the opening of the new yard at Kingmoor in 1963. Another casualty of the 1959–60 period was an almost unknown single track spur that ran from Gretna Junction on the Caley main line to Longtown on the Waverley Route. This route, known locally as the 'Guards Mill spur', was closed as a through-route on 18 July 1960. One of its main functions was to serve a series of goods sidings into the vast Naval Ordnance depôts and explosive stores on the flat marshy ground east of Mossband and for three years these were still served by a shunting service from the Gretna end. When the up goods spur from Longtown Junction to Kingmoor Yard was brought into use

115 The new signal box and colour light signals at the south end of Citadel Station on 23 July 1952.

early in 1963 the Ordnance depôt sidings were served from this new line and the connection at Gretna removed.

Undoubtedly the most important recent event in the railway history of Carlisle has been the construction of the great new marshalling yards at Kingmoor. Work on this project started in 1959 and was completed in 1963. The yard was opened in stages, the up side on 25 March 1963 and the down side on 17 June 1963. The basic principle of the yard was to keep the up and down traffic separated as far as possible and to this end the yard was more or less halved. Up traffic (that from Scotland) was handled on the east side by means of up reception sidings of eight lines, then a massive block of forty-eight sorting sidings and finally a block of ten departure sidings. Down traffic was similarly catered for on the west side with ten down reception sidings, thirty-seven sorting sidings and ten departure sidings. Between these two halves there were facilities for the machines – two control towers, a small shed and various sidings for the diesel shunters that worked the yard, plus space for main-line locomotives to wait while their trains were re-marshalled. There were also amenity facilities for the men who worked in the yard. Finally there was an avoiding line around the extreme west side of the yard complex that was used for through goods trains and also for passenger train diversions when the main line was being relayed. In addition to the yard control towers, a new signal box was built near the bridge carrying the Waverley Route over the old Caledonian main line. This box, apart from controlling the entries and exits from the new marshalling yard, also covered the main line from Caldew Junction to Floriston in the first instance, and ultimately to Gretna. In addition, it controlled the movements into the old Kingmoor M.P.D. and the new diesel depôt as well as the new up goods loop from Longtown. One result of the introduction of the new box was the immediate closing of boxes at Etterby Bridge and Rockcliffe Station. The new power box at Kingmoor is destined to have an even shorter life than its equivalent at Carlisle No. 5, as it also is to vanish with the new signalling arrangements resulting from the Anglo/Scottish electrification in 1974. The two towers controlling shunting movements in the yard, however, are to remain.

Between Kingmoor Yard and the Scottish Border, fairly extensive alterations were needed to serve the new yard. The new goods line from Longtown to Kingmoor has already been mentioned but this in turn entailed the widening of the viaduct over the River Esk at Metalbridge to take three lines (one down and two up). To do this the old typical Caley bridge of plate girders on stone piers had to be nearly completely rebuilt in pre-stressed concrete. This work started in 1958 and was completed two years later. The other major engineering structure was a fly-over carrying the up goods lines into the new marshalling yard. This was also constructed in pre-stressed concrete and carried the goods line across the up and down Caledonian main line. At the same time these goods lines were carried out as far as Floriston level-crossing where the down lines converged. On the up side, a cross-over fed into the up main, while the third line continued on to Longtown, leaving the Caley line near the site of Mossband signal box and bearing away eastward serving the various Ordnance sidings on its way. Once Kingmoor New Yard was in operation, Mossband signal box was closed and demolished. The other signal box affected by this

116 The final stage of rebuilding the Esk Viaduct at Mossband. The contrast with a Duchess on the same bridge in earlier days (Plate 90) is a fitting comment on the aesthetic tastes of this century!

track triplication was Floriston and here the pattern is more complicated. Floriston box also controlled a level-crossing and so, though it lost its signalling functions with the opening of the new Kingmoor box in 1963, it was retained as a crossing-keeper's box till 23 May 1970. But not without a break, for on 17 September 1967 automatic half-barriers were installed and for a period the crossing-keeper was withdrawn. After the Hixon Crossing disaster a crossing-keeper was re-instated till 23 May 1970. The box was finally demolished on 4 October 1970.

South of the new yard, several extensive track alterations were made necessary. The most important of these was a completely new double-tracked spur from Canal Junction (the signal box where the Silloth Branch diverged from the Waverley Route) to the east end of the new yard. This gave a second freight route round Citadel Station by linking with the existing goods lines from Rome Street Junction to Canal Junction. With the closing of the Waverley Route and also of the steam shed at Kingmoor, this spur was closed in 1969 and Canal box closed on 3 August 1969. The other interesting track layout from the new yard was the line to serve down goods traffic on to the Waverley Route. This started out from the west side of the yard in a southerly direction and joined the old Waverley Route at a loop near Stainton level-crossing. Here all trains for Edinburgh had to change direction and the locomotive had to run round, as propelling out of the yard was not permitted. Strange to say, despite the closing of the Waverley Route on 6 January 1969, this spur is still used occasionally for goods workings to the R.A.F. depôt at Brunthill sidings, immediately west of the old Harker Station.

The construction of the new yard at Kingmoor must have been the largest civil engineering operation undertaken in the Carlisle area for many years and the ballasting alone necessitated the running of special trains daily for nearly two years. Some of the ballast for the yard came from the quarries of North Yorkshire over the Settle and Carlisle line, but the bulk came from the quarries at Sandside on the branch line from Arnside which is on the Furness line to Hincaster Junction on the L.N.W.R. It was this traffic that gave the Hincaster spur, as the line was known locally, an extended lease of life. A very heavy train left Sandside in the mid-afternoon and worked to Tebay where it stabled over-night leaving for Carlisle again at 6 a.m. Tebay had two Austerity 2–8–0s stabled there for working these trains, and the Carlisle-bound one on an early summer's morning made a splendid sight as it climbed Shap, all-out from a cold start with one and often two bankers behind. Almost more spectacular, however, was the first leg of the journey from Sandside, as after crossing the unique viaduct across the Bela River near Heversham village on the A6, there was a short stretch of formidable grade through rather narrow damp cuttings that often reduced the Austerity to a state of slipping impotence. The rails mostly came from the U.S. Company at Workington over the Maryport and Carlisle.

The completion of Kingmoor New Yard in June 1963 gave rise to a considerable rationalisation of freight workings round the Border City and resulted in the closure of some of the smaller, and not so small, goods yards. The first casualty was the Midland yard at Durranhill which was immediately closed and the tracks lifted by the end of the year. The old L.N.W.R. yard at Crown Street, immediately south of Citadel Station on the east side, also went about this time and the connecting spur that weaved its way over and under more important lines between there and Upperby was lifted. North of Citadel, the Viaduct yard of the Caley was also phased out – all the goods traffic for Carlisle being concentrated at Dentonholme yard, served by a short branch of the goods lines at Dentonholme North Junction. This still survives since Kingmoor does not load or unload any traffic for (or originating from) the Carlisle district. This is worked out instead from Dentonholme by shunting services. Notwithstanding these closures, the end of 1963 probably saw the lines in and around Carlisle at their most complex. But the shadow of Beeching was large upon the scene and closures were soon to come: resulting in a contraction of layout, though not of traffic as, if anything, freight traffic has increased over the past few years – though of a very different type to when the new marshalling yard was first projected.

The first of the closures that had much bearing on train-working round Carlisle affected the passenger side more than the freight. On Sunday, 5 September 1964, the branch to Silloth ran its last train – the final one returning in a blaze of notoriety with persons sitting on the track and only being removed by policemen with dogs. The story of the Silloth Branch is a strange one and a complete reversal of the normal pattern of branch railways. When built, great hopes were placed on its importance as a line for shipping goods from the Carlisle area through the port of Silloth. But these never materialised and before the line finally closed, goods traffic was down to a trickle. In its last years, however, it carried a considerable seasonal passenger traffic to the great sand beaches round Silloth, and even as late as 1963 it was not uncommon to see J 37 class 0–6–0s staggering along the branch with eight packed coaches on a summer Sunday morning. Another closure of the early 1960s

117 A splendid view of the City from Etterby Bridge with Britannia No. 72003 *Clan Fraser* heading a Carlisle–Glasgow express parcels.

was the spur from Bog Junction on the goods lines to Forks Junction (Carlisle No. 9) on the M. & C.R. This spur, though disconnected, had the track left down and there is a rumour that it may be re-opened shortly for through-trains from the North East to West Cumberland, which at the moment have to run out to Kingmoor New Yard and reverse.

If the closure of the Silloth Branch had little effect on the train-working and lay-out of Carlisle district, then the next closure most certainly had. The old North British Waverley Route to Hawick and Edinburgh closed on 6 February 1969. This meant the immediate loss of four stopping trains to and from Edinburgh, plus two through-workings to St Pancras over the S. & C.R. and the odd local train to Hawick – not to mention the morning and afternoon workers trains to Harker for the nearby R.A.F. depôt. If anything, the effect on freight traffic was more drastic, for even as late as the summer of 1968 the Waverley Route had six or seven heavily loaded freights each day. Immediately after the closure of the Waverley Route the connections of the Caley main line at Carlisle No. 2 Junction were cut and lifted. The box has subsequently been demolished. For eight months Canal Junction signal box remained, dealing only with trains round the goods line from Rome Street (Carlisle No. 11) to Kingmoor New Yard via the new spur. This box was closed in its turn on 3 August 1969 and the spur to the new yard disconnected. By this time Kingmoor M.P.D., the steam shed to the east of the main line, had closed and the lack of light engine movements enabled all freight traffic bypassing Citadel to be routed from Rome Street to Kingmoor by way of Dentonholme North Junction. A single line from the new yard to the sidings at Brunthill is now all that remains of the Waverley Route, and irony is added to its eclipse by the fact that a few yards of the formation immediately north of the old Harker Station now forms part of the motorway that bypasses Carlisle. Another casualty of the Waverley Route closure was the new up goods line from Longtown to Kingmoor. This no longer had any reason to exist as a through-route, but has been retained to serve the Ordnance sidings near Mossband with a remote-controlled crossing near the site of the old Floriston box to let shunting trains on to and off the main line. These sidings are worked as tablet locked sidings as and when required. Few lines in British railway history can have had a shorter life than the up goods line from Longtown to Kingmoor or, come to that, the spur from Canal Junction to the south end of the new yard.

The phasing out of the steam locomotive also left its melancholy mark on the railways of Carlisle in other ways. I have mentioned the closure of the Midland shed at Durranhill in 1959, or early 1960, and the transfer of the locomotives from there to Upperby. But even Upperby did not survive to see the end of steam, for as the use of diesel electrics increased, the tendency was to concentrate Carlisle's remaining steam power at Kingmoor. On 1 January 1968, Upperby depôt closed, though it remained for a time as a stabling point for D.M.U.s. For two years before the official closure, Upperby had seen little main-line steam working, being used mainly as a refuge for steam locomotives 'in store' but never likely to work again. However, it did have its blaze of glory at the time when electrification of the Crewe–Euston line was incomplete and the new diesels were not behaving too well. Some of the best of Carlisle's Britannia Pacifics and a few of its class 5s were stored there in case of dire emergency. Among those to be stored was No. 70013 *Oliver Cromwell* which was to be B.R.'s last Pacific. *Oliver Cromwell* was destined to play the concluding act in the steam saga of Carlisle when on Sunday, 11 August 1968, it worked B.R.'s

118 The train arrival board at Citadel Station in 1937; which rather emphasises the lowly role of the mighty North Eastern at Carlisle.

last steam excursion from Liverpool to Carlisle over the Settle and Carlisle line. This train returned a few minutes later behind two of Stanier's classic Black 5 4–6–0s and the age of steam in Carlisle was over!

The end of steam had other far-reaching effects on the railways of Carlisle. The old Caledonian steam sheds at Kingmoor were closed and the maintenance of diesel locomotives transferred to a new depôt built on the other side of the main line to the north. This depôt was devoted to servicing and maintenance rather than stabling of locomotives, for with complete dieselisation the need for Carlisle to supply fresh engines from its own stud had gone. Of the very few locomotives officially based at the new Kingmoor depôt, most are shunters or diesels of a lower order for working local freight traffic. At the present time diesels work in, are fueled, on occasions put through the washing plant, re-manned and sent on their way again. What electrification will bring remains to be seen, but if Crewe's experience is anything to go by, the new depôt at Kingmoor will be used increasingly as a shed dealing with diesels for local working and trains over the section only, plus D.M.U.s for local stopping services. Upperby shed was in an even worse plight for it had been closed to main-line workings eight months before the end of steam, and latterly used only for storing condemned steam engines plus the maintenance of D.M.U.s for the Keswick and West Cumberland services. At the time of writing, all the D.M.U. maintenance is concentrated at Kingmoor diesel depôt and much of Upperby yard has been lifted, but what is left is to be used as an electrification depôt. Once this work is completed it will presumably be closed completely.

It is clear that there have been more changes in the railways of Carlisle in the past twenty years than in the preceding fifty. However, now that electrification of the West Coast main line has started north of Crewe, there are greater and from a human aspect, more significant, changes to come. The most far reaching of these changes will be in the signalling, and already the foundations of a new power signal box are taking shape behind the 'new' (1953) No. 5 box. This signal box will control everything from Carnforth to Kirkpatrick over the Scottish Border, including the goods lines and the entrance and exits to Kingmoor marshalling yard. Once this is completed, every other signal box in the Carlisle numbering system will be closed, not to mention all the ones on the L.N.W.R./Caledonian main lines. Facilities for electric locomotive working will be introduced in Kingmoor New Yard, though the shunting and marshalling of trains will still be done by diesel shunters. Another alarming shadow cast by electrification is the closure of the Settle and Carlisle line with its graceful viaducts and long dank tunnels – all of which are engineering wonders, but costly to maintain. The S. & C.R. may remain as long as there are short-wheelbased wagons, but after that its future looks non-existent. The recent development of bulk company trains from Teeside to West Cumberland and the Ayrshire coast have probably saved the Newcastle–Carlisle and G.S.W.R. lines from extinction, also the Maryport and Carlisle.

From a passenger point of view, Carlisle's importance was as an interchange point and the fewer the lines left to serve it, the less will be the scope for traffic from this source. It is far from being beyond the bounds of possibility that the end of this decade will see non-stop trains from London to Glasgow in four hours which will slow to a modest 75 m.p.h. through Citadel as they already do through Rugby! Certainly there will be passenger traffic, but it will lack the glamour of crack expresses stopping and changing locomotives that gave Citadel its unique aura in steam days and which has still managed to survive the diesel era. Its freight traffic has a more critical importance and electrification may well increase this, when the great modern yard at Kingmoor becomes the marshalling yard for Southern Scotland, replacing many old and inconvenient yards round the industrial outskirts of Glasgow. But one thing is sure, Carlisle by its geographical nature, occupied a unique position in Britain's railways and thus generated a mystique all of its own – whether behind an A6 or a Webb compound, to arrive at Citadel is like crossing the border into a different country, which in many ways one is.

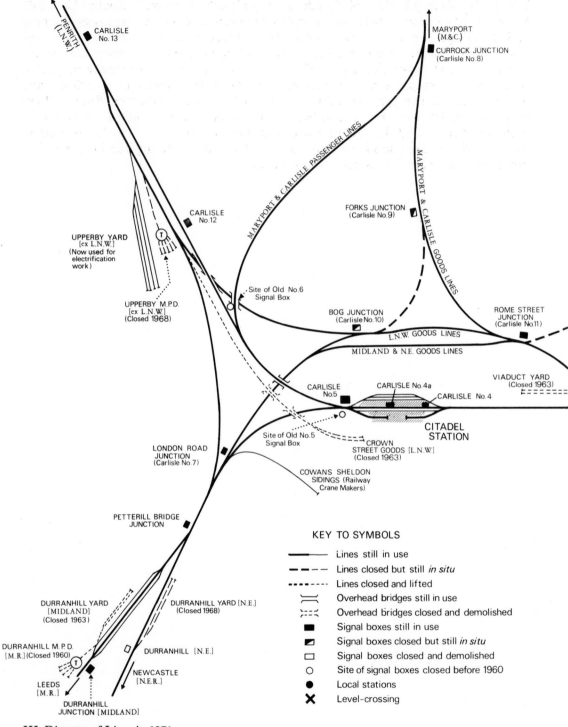

PENRITH (L.N.W.)

CARLISLE No. 13

MARYPORT (M&C.)

CURROCK JUNCTION (Carlisle No.8)

UPPERBY YARD [ex L.N.W.] (Now used for electrification work)

CARLISLE No.12

FORKS JUNCTION (Carlisle No.9)

MARYPORT & CARLISLE PASSENGER LINES

MARYPORT & CARLISLE GOODS LINES

UPPERBY M.P.D. [ex L.N.W.] (Closed 1968)

Site of Old No.6 Signal Box

BOG JUNCTION (Carlisle No.10)

ROME STREET JUNCTION (Carlisle No.11)

L.N.W. GOODS LINES

MIDLAND & N.E. GOODS LINES

VIADUCT YARD (Closed 1963)

CARLISLE No.5

CARLISLE No. 4a

CARLISLE No. 4

CITADEL STATION

Site of Old No.5 Signal Box

CROWN STREET GOODS [L.N.W.] (Closed 1963)

LONDON ROAD JUNCTION (Carlisle No.7)

COWANS SHELDON SIDINGS (Railway Crane Makers)

PETTERILL BRIDGE JUNCTION

DURRANHILL YARD [MIDLAND] (Closed 1963)

DURRANHILL YARD [N.E.] (Closed 1968)

DURRANHILL M.P.D. [M.R.] (Closed 1960)

DURRANHILL [N.E.]

LEEDS [M.R.]

NEWCASTLE [N.E.R.]

DURRANHILL JUNCTION [MIDLAND]

KEY TO SYMBOLS

———	Lines still in use
– – –	Lines closed but still *in situ*
·······	Lines closed and lifted
⌣	Overhead bridges still in use
⌣	Overhead bridges closed and demolished
■	Signal boxes still in use
◨	Signal boxes closed but still *in situ*
□	Signal boxes closed and demolished
○	Site of signal boxes closed before 1960
●	Local stations
✕	Level-crossing

III Diagram of Lines in 1971

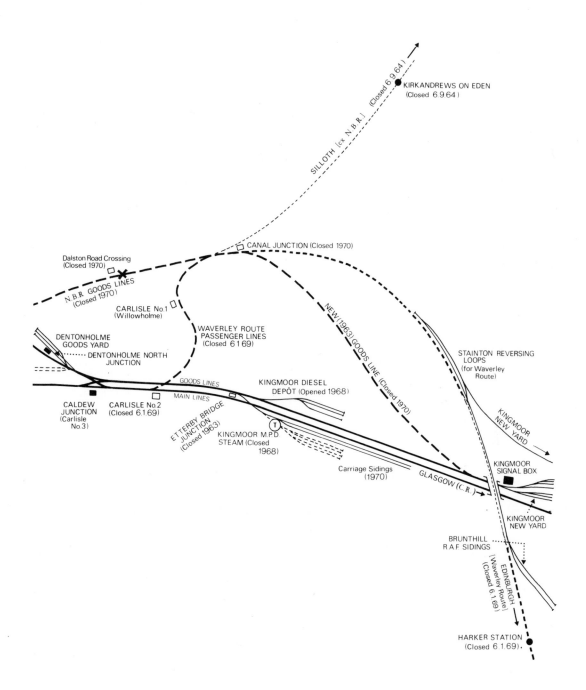

KIRKANDREWS ON EDEN
(Closed 6.9.64.)

SILLOTH (ex N.B.R.) (Closed 6.9.64.)

CANAL JUNCTION (Closed 1970)

Dalston Road Crossing
(Closed 1970)

N.B.R GOODS LINES
(Closed 1970)

CARLISLE No.1
(Willowholme)

NEW (1963) GOODS LINE (Closed 1970)

DENTONHOLME
GOODS YARD

DENTONHOLME NORTH
JUNCTION

WAVERLEY ROUTE
PASSENGER LINES
(Closed 6.1.69)

STAINTON REVERSING
LOOPS
(for Waverley
Route)

GOODS LINES

KINGMOOR DIESEL
DEPÔT (Opened 1968)

MAIN LINES

KINGMOOR
NEW YARD

CALDEW
JUNCTION
(Carlisle
No.3)

CARLISLE No.2
(Closed 6.1.69)

ETTERBY BRIDGE
JUNCTION
(Closed 1963)

KINGMOOR M.P.D.
STEAM (Closed
1968)

Carriage Sidings
(1970)

GLASGOW (C.R.)

KINGMOOR
SIGNAL BOX

KINGMOOR
NEW YARD

BRUNTHILL
R.A.F. SIDINGS

EDINBURGH
(Waverley Route)
(Closed 6.1.69)

HARKER STATION
(Closed 6.1.69.)

APPENDIXES

Appendix 1

List of signal boxes around Carlisle with their official L.M.S.R./B.R. numbers which were seldom used and their older names which were.

Official No.	Name	Position	Recent History
No. 1	Willowholme Junction.	N.B.R. goods yard control.	Demolished at time of closure of the Waverley Route.
No. 2	None.	—	—
No. 3	Caldew Junction.	Junction of Waverley Route and Caley M/L.	Still open but Waverley Route connections lifted.
No. 4	None.	Immediately north of Citadel Station.	Still in use.
No. 4a	None.	In buildings above Station to control movements within Citadel Station.	Still in use.
No. 5	None.	South of Citadel on west side. Replaced old No. 5 and No. 6.	Still in use but to be replaced by new box for electrification.
No. 6	Unknown.	Box in junction of M. & C.R. and L.N.W.R. lines south of Citadel.	Closed and demolished in 1953.
No. 7	London Road Junction.	S.W. of junction between S. & C.R. and N.E.R. lines into Citadel and spur to L.N.W.R. yard at Upperby. Also controlled access to goods lines.	Still in use.
No. 8	Currock Junction.	Where M. & C.R. line from Citadel joins goods line from K.N.Y. and Rome Street.	Still in use.
No. 9	Forks Junctions.	Where spur from Bog Junction joins goods lines to the M. & C.R. (spur disconnected).	Out of use but box still stands.
No. 10	Bog Junction.	Where goods lines from L.N.W.R. and Midland/N.E.R. met and spur to M. & C.R. took off.	Closed but box still stands.
No. 11	Rome Street Junction.	On goods lines where line from M. & C.R. joined those from the south. Also where goods line to N.B.R. at Canal Junction left.	Open but line to Canal Junction disconnected.
No. 12	Upperby Junction.	At junction of L.N.W. main line and spur from N.E.R. at London Road. Also controlled access to Upperby M.P.D.	Still in use.

No. 13	Upperby Bridge Junction.	At south end of Upperby M.P.D.	Still in use.
–	Peterill Bridge Junction.	Where N.E.R. and S. & C.R. lines met.	Still in use.
–	Durranhill Junction.	On Midland that used to control Durranhill yard and M.P.D.	Still in use.
–	Durranhill N.E.	On N.E.R. that used to control their yard.	Closed and demolished.

Appendix 2

List of Events

Autumn 1952	Closure of Floriston Station.
Feb./Mar. 1953	New No. 5 signal box commissioned, replaces old No. 5 box and No. 6 box south of Citadel Station. Semaphore signals in the Station area replaced by coloured lights.
1958	Overall Station roof removed from all but central section of Citadel. Old supporting walls on each side left.
1959	Construction of Kingmoor New Yard commenced.
Late 1959 or early 1960	Durranhill locomotive sheds closed.
18 July 1960	Guards Mill spur from Gretna Junction to Longtown closed as a through-route, sidings to R.N. Ordnance Depôts at Mossband worked from Gretna end till July 1963.
1958/60	Rebuilding of viaduct over River Esk at Metalbridge to take an extra track, the up-goods line from Longtown to K.N.Y. In actual fact this was in use as a relief line from Mossband box to Rockcliffe for two years before the opening of the new yard.
17 Feb. 1963	Floriston box closed other than to work level-crossing.
25 March 1963	Completion of up side of Kingmoor New Yard.
Early 1963	Rockcliffe Station closed completely after being used for some years for workers trains to the nearby R.A.F. depôt.
17 June 1963	Completion of down side of Kingmoor New Yard.
Summer 1963	Closure of Durranhill yard (ex Midland).
Autumn 1963	Closure of Crown Street Goods (ex L.N.W.R.). In both cases track and approach roads lifted soon after. New goods line from Longtown to Kingmoor in use. Naval Ordnance sidings worked from Gretna transferred to this line and Gretna connection closed. Mossband signal box closed and demolished. New goods line from Canal Junction to K.N.Y. in use.
17 June 1963	Floriston closed as a signal box. Remains open for level-crossing.
6 Sept. 1963	Official closing of Silloth Branch. Last trains ran the previous day (Sunday). Track lifted immediately.
17 Sept. 1967	Automatic half-barrier crossing in operation at Floriston Crossing. Keeper withdrawn for a short while then reinstated after the Hixon Crossing disaster.
1 Jan. 1968	All steam locomotive allocation at Carlisle withdrawn. Upperby M.P.D. closed to main line locomotive working but still used for storing condemned locomotives for a few months and as a D.M.U. maintenance point.
11 Aug. 1968	Last B.R. steam train runs from Liverpool to Carlisle and back via the S. & C.
Autumn 1968	New diesel depôt in use at Kingmoor. Track lifted from old Kingmoor steam shed though some sidings retained for storing coaches. Old shed still standing (March 1971).

6 Jan. 1969   Closure of Waverley Route apart from short length to Brunthill sidings for R.A.F. traffic. Local workers trains to Harker withdrawn. Closure of up goods loop from Longtown to K.N.Y. other than as a tablet locked siding for Ordnance traffic to and from the R.N. stores at Mossband. Connections at Caldew Junction severed. Canal Junction retained only for operating the new spur to Kingmoor New Yard.

13 May 1970   Crossing-keeper finally withdrawn from Floriston.

Summer 1970   New spur from Canal Junction to K.N.Y. disconnected but track still in place (March 1970). Goods line from Canal Junction to Rome Street (Carlisle No. 11) taken out of use. Canal Junction signal box closed. Dalston Road crossing box closed (this was where the goods lines crossed the main West Cumberland road). Bog Junction signal box closed.

4 Oct. 1970   Floriston signal/crossing-keeper's box demolished.

Jan. 1971   Start made on building new power box behind 'new' No. 5 for re-signalling in connection with electrification.

Index